LOST BOYS

REFLECTIONS ON PSYCHOANALYSIS AND COUNTERTRANSFERENCE

LOST BOYS

REFLECTIONS ON PSYCHOANALYSIS
AND COUNTERTRANSFERENCE

Frederick H. Berenstein

W.W. NORTON & COMPANY · NEW YORK · LONDON

Library of Congress Cataloging-in-Publication Data

Berenstein, Frederick H.
    Lost boys : reflections on psychoanalysis and countertransference
/ Frederick H. Berenstein.
        p.   cm.
    "A Norton professional book".
    ISBN 0-393-70188-3
    1. Child analysis—Case studies.   2. Countertransference
(Psychology)—Case studies.   I. Title.
RJ504.B44   1995
618.92'8917—dc20   94-45955   CIP

        W. W. Norton & Company, Inc., 500 Fifth Avenue, New York, NY 10110
        W. W. Norton & Company, Ltd., 10 Coptic Street, London WC1A 1PU

1   2   3   4   5   6   7   8   9   0

To my wife, Robin, and my family, who constantly refilled my reservoir of love.

And to the children whose endless hope and longing guided them to share in it.

Contents

Foreword

Mira Rothenberg

Rick Berenstein is a wonderful human being and a remarkable analyst. His love and compassion for "his children" seem limitless. His intelligence, humility, understanding of and sensitivity to these children are vast, and the delicacy with which he uses all these qualities is profound.

With the agility of an acrobat he weaves in and out of these children's fairy tales. And when the child seems ready to try and venture into reality—thus stepping out of his fairy tale, if only for a little while—Rick is there with him. They do it together. For example, read the story of "The Snow Leopard."

The depth of Rick's understanding of the child's psyche is great, as so painfully but clearly seen in his sense of the true meaning of the short story written by Peter (Chapter 1 appendix).

His imagination, his honesty, and his respect for the

child's rage, hurt, and love can be seen in every chapter of this book, especially clearly, in my mind, in the story of Alex, "On the Importance of Moving Slowly." This is a most impressive chapter since the child writes it himself. He describes what an analyst should be like and in his own words details Rick's treatment of him.

Each chapter in this book tells of a different child's experience of his life's story, and his analytic healing. But each story in this book tells of the same childhood experience—of pain, rage, hopelessness, and destroyed love and eventual healing. Rick does not just write about "his children" and their treatment, but he lives their stories with them—with untiring devotion. And they write too, about themselves, about their treatment by Rick, and about Rick.

Lost Boys is a most unusual book. It gives us glimpses into a child's soul with such clarity, even if with agony, but it leaves us with love. It gives us a glimpse of the tremendous complexity of the child's soul and it leaves us with a dignity and respect for it.

It is a privilege to watch this unweaving of the human spider web that both Rick and "his children," almost equally, participate in.

Acknowledgments

I am very glad to have the opportunity to thank the following friends and colleagues who took time out from their busy schedules to read these chapters and send me their thoughtful criticisms and corrections: Mr. Norman Alexander, Mr. Fred Bever, Dr. Judy Corkum, the late Dr. Elisabeth Enczi, the late Dr. Gladys Fitzpatrick, Dr. Norman Klein, Ms. Ann O'Grady, the late Dr. Virginia Pomeranz, Ms. Mira Rothenberg, Dr. Jose Szapocznik, and Dr. Wanda Willig.

Preface

One of my friends urged me to write a preface for this book to explain, however briefly, my psychoanalytic beliefs or at least why I do what I do. I can, I hope, if called on, back up my beliefs with theoretical formulations in which I have faith.[1] But, in common with Einstein, my boyhood hero, I have very little faith in theories, having seen too often how we become attached to them and then cannot give them up, even when it becomes clear that they are no longer adequate. Besides, each child has his own life, and thus *his own theory*; the child should make the theory and not the other way around. Those who are fa-

[1]Bowlby's work on attachment and loss, E. Becker's seminal books (especially *The Denial of Death*), the developmental work of Margaret Mahler and her associates, S. and Anna Freud, the later works of Bettelheim (especially *Freud and Man's Soul*), R. D. Laing, K. Horney, Kohut, the Kernbergs, D. W. Winnicott.

miliar with the writers mentioned below will catch, I hope, glimpses of them in the pages that follow. For those who are not, however, the main thing is to catch the image of the children, for that is what this book is really about.

None of the children in this book were born lost. Rather they became lost as children usually do, when they wander away from their parents (to what?) or are abandoned. It was my great fortune to have them, and so many others, come into my life and make me better than I was before. By honoring the promises they needed me to make—to be there always, caring, listening, loving, accepting—they came to trust again, grow again, and love again, and they brought me to see the depth of my character, my longing for them (and myself), and the miraculous abundance of loving of which we are all capable.

For those who are parents, or who may someday become them, let this book be a warning. Cherish your children, nourish them, let them grow into themselves by accepting and loving who they are. You will slip and fail sometimes as we all must, and yet, push on again. Look at them as they really are—the wonders of creation. And, on a day when you lose sight of that vision and want it back, step away, just for a moment, look carefully, deeply, and ask yourself:

> What if I had never seen this before?
> What if I knew I would never see it again?[2]

[2]Carson, R. *The Sense of Wonder*. New York: Harper & Row, 1956, p. 52.

Introduction

The central questions in psychoanalysis are: What has happened to the children who come to us? What force can bend the natural flow of human development from growth to the illogical, self-defeating, and ultimately self-destructive behaviors we see in our work every day? If only we knew the answer, perhaps we would know what to do to help.

One way to approach this question is to wonder what infants are really like. We know that human infants are utterly dependent at birth and for a long time after. Margaret Mahler,[1] who has closely followed the psychological development of children from birth onward, describes the state of the infant from birth to about four or five months

[1]Mahler, M. "On the First Three Subphases of the Separation-Individuation Process." *Int. J. of Psycho-Analysis*, 1972, *53*, pp. 333–338.

as a symbiotic phase, wherein the mother-infant pair exists and works, at least from the infant's point of view, as one. The infant does not, and probably cannot, clearly differentiate itself from the mother, i.e., it cannot clearly see that the mother and itself are separate beings.

Ernest Becker, in *The Denial of Death*, sees this situation as the wellspring of the anxiety that is a fundamental feature of the human condition. He writes that from birth the child "is absolutely dependent on the mother, experiences loneliness when she is absent, frustration when he is deprived of gratification, irritation at hunger and discomfort, and so on. If he were abandoned to himself his world would drop away, and his organism must sense this at some level . . . this anxiety, then, is a natural, organismic fear of annihilation."[2]

But, of course, in most cases the child's world does not drop away. His[3] needs are met by competent, loving parents. In this caring environment he grows, in his first five years, increasingly toward separation and individuation. The first tentative explorations away from his caregivers are rewarded by the joy of discovery and the permanence of the parents when he returns to them. This leads to the secure feelings that allow further and greater explorations.

But what if the infant is not met by tender, loving hands? What if the hand that feeds is also the hand that abuses? What if the voice that soothes alternates unpre-

[2]Becker, E. *The Denial of Death*. New York: Free Press, 1973, p. 13.

[3]For the sake of simplicity, and because this is a book about boys, only the masculine pronoun is used in the text.

dictably with the voice that shrieks? What if the love that was once there suddenly disappears?

The child is thrown back to the primitive fear of annihilation. At least on the organismic level of which Becker speaks, he must be terrified. It is impossible to live with such anxiety. The mind springs into action to save the child; the defense mechanisms are born.

Inevitably, however, the defense mechanisms outlive their value. The child grows older and more competent. He is no longer realistically on the brink of destruction, yet the defenses refuse to die. Not in touch clearly with the real world, the defenses insist that if they are abandoned death will follow. The terror of this possibility gives them continued life at a terrible price; little by little they get in the way of a child's development, isolating him from reality and the warmth of other human beings.

From this point of view, we see why therapy that seeks only to understand and interpret is doomed to fail with such children. Understanding and interpretation only address the defense mechanisms. But if the analyst offers nothing else, the child has no compelling reason to give them up. If he did, he would be forced to face his original terror—and this he cannot do.

The analyst must also address the failure of nurturance. He must come to care for each child, to give each child the secure feeling that he is loved. Only when this is done will the child feel safe enough to abandon the crippling defenses. Then the understanding and interpreting will help to guide him in his efforts. Without love this is not possible.

When we ask a child in therapy to trust us, we must

never forget that, for the child who has trusted and been badly hurt, we are asking for the most incredible leap of faith. And what can we offer in return? That we will be there for them, really care, genuinely love. The child who comes to believe that we truly care will open himself up to love and to loving other people. Every child who has been badly hurt before eventually asks, in his own way, "Do you love me?" It is the analyst's work to find his way to that private place, to be ready and waiting to catch the child in his strong arms when the child finally makes the leap into the void.

you may say I'm a dreamer, but I'm not the only one

imagine, John Lennon

1

THE SNOW LEOPARD

Fusion in an Elaborated Delusional Fantasy

There's a place for us, somewhere a place for us,
Peace and quiet and open air, wait for us . . . somewhere.
There's a time for us, someday a time for us,
Time together with time to spare, time to look, time to care.
Someday, somewhere, we'll find a new way of living;
We'll find a way of forgiving . . . someday.
There's a place for us, a time and place for us.
Hold my hand and we're half-way there;
Hold my hand and I'll take you there,
Somehow . . . someday . . . somewhere.

"Somewhere," from West Side Story

This chapter is a clinical summary of my work and my
relationship, over a period of many years, with a boy

named Peter who initially presented himself as a snow leopard living in the Himalayas. It is, in the end, a story about an immensely talented young man and his battle to come back to reality from fantasy. It is also, I realize, a story about the fusion of therapist and patient and about the difficulties that this created for me as well as for Peter; it is as much about my weaknesses as about his, as much about my strength as about his.

Peter was initially referred by his pediatrician after an incident in which he had accidentally broken the collarbone of his three-year-old half-brother. When Peter and his parents (actually his mother and stepfather) first walked into my office, it was difficult to tell if Peter was a boy; his face, body shape, and hair seemed completely androgynous. He sat quietly near to me while his mother sketched out the details of his life. He had been the first child of her first marriage. She had left her first husband and Peter abruptly when Peter was five years old in order to join her present husband, who was at that time her lover. Peter had continued to live with his father for a few years, visiting his mother and stepfather on vacations.

Not long after leaving her first husband, Mrs. S. discovered that she was pregnant. Initially it appeared that the baby was Mr. and Mrs. S.'s first offspring, but it turned out that the baby was Peter's real brother. Mrs. S. and her new husband decided that they did not want to start out their new family with someone else's (?!) child, and placed the baby in an adoption nursery. They informed Mr. O., Peter's father, of the birth and he offered

---

This chapter is dedicated to the memory of my friend and colleague, Dr. Elisabeth Enczi, who first suggested that it be written.

to take the baby and raise him, along with Peter, rather than have him put up for adoption. This was tentatively agreed to, Mr. O. thought, and during the next winter vacation he sent Peter off to visit his mother and his new baby brother.

In subsequent sessions it became clear that boarding a plane with a rattle for his new baby brother was one of Peter's earliest memories. However, when Peter arrived in the country in which his mother and stepfather were living, he did not meet his new sibling. Instead Mrs. S. wrote to Peter's father and demanded that he sign the adoption papers or else she would not send Peter back. Faced with the choice of the child he knew and loved and the baby he had never met, Mr. O. chose Peter and signed the adoption papers.

Although Mrs. S. did not reveal this in Peter's presence, the reason, ostensibly, that she did not want Mr. O. to have the baby was that she had left Mr. O. because of his extramarital homosexual affairs. In a subsequent telephone conversation she detailed this, along with her concern that Peter might be a homosexual. Peter was twelve years old at the time.

After Peter returned to his father, Mr. and Mrs. S. returned to the United States and instigated a suit to gain custody of Peter. In the ensuing court battle, of which I later received voluminous documents, Mr. O.'s bisexuality seems to have been the major bone of contention. Peter was examined, at length, by a number of specialists to determine if he was homosexual or extremely effeminate. He was six years old at the time.

Custody was finally awarded to Peter's mother, and Peter joined her and his stepfather in a foreign country.

After four years, they returned to the United States. They had had two sons of their own. Peter's father had also remarried by the time Peter returned from abroad. That remarriage eventually produced yet another half-brother and half-sister for Peter.

Peter visited with his father every Christmas, Easter, and summer vacation; he had, in fact, just returned from such a visit when the incident that led to his referral occurred.

During the relating of all of this background material, Peter sat quietly staring at me. His enormous green eyes looked longingly through his large mop of dirty blond hair.

I took Mr. and Mrs. S. out to the waiting room, and then went back to talk to Peter alone. He talked so gently and quietly; the accident with his half-brother obviously was very painful to him. He was clearly an extremely bright child, but evidenced pseudo-retardation, claiming, for example, to be unable to spell his stepfather's five-letter last name ("I don't use it. I have trouble spelling it."). And, at twelve, he was still sleeping with a teddy bear (a transitional object) to whom he told all his troubles. He was doing poorly in a very top level private school where he had had to repeat fourth grade on his return from abroad because of his poor English.

Peter and I quickly established a very sympathetic rapport. By the end of the first session I felt comfortable enough to ask him if he could tell me honestly whether he would rather be a girl or a boy. He replied that he would rather be a girl.

Between that first session and the second I felt that I

could see my work cut out for me. How wrong I was. When Peter returned, and the subject of his gender preference came up, he said, "It doesn't really matter." When I suggested that it did to most people, Peter said, "But I'm not a person."

"If you're not a person," I said, "then what are you?"

And Peter replied, "I'm a snow leopard. I live in the Himalayas."

The next day I went to the library to see what I could learn about snow leopards. I felt sure that I would never meet face to face with the real Peter in any other way than by joining him where he was and as he believed himself to be. The sum total of what I was able to find in the library, however, was quite meager. The snow leopard is a beautiful, usually all white, member of the leopard family. Its natural habitat is the Himalayas, above the eight thousand foot level, and it is a loner except when mating. After mating the male does not stay around to provide for the litter. The snow leopard is the king of the mountain; the species is almost extinct. It seemed very improbable that Peter, who was only twelve, could have created much of a delusion with so little material. Years later, however, when I compared my notes with Peter Matthiessen's description of the snow leopard,[1] I was struck by how much Peter knew about the habits of the animal.

Nevertheless, on the surface it appeared that Peter had picked an extremely appropriate delusion for himself. With his mane of dirty blond hair and green eyes, he looked a good deal like a cat. In this world he was a

[1]Matthiessen, Peter. *The Snow Leopard*. New York: Viking, 1978.

frightened little boy, uncertain of his gender; in that world he was definitely male and lord of all he surveyed. In both worlds he was almost extinct.

In our first few months together our sessions developed a pattern. Peter usually seemed quite happy to be with me and would talk quietly about his school and home life. But any attempt at interpretation or trying to help him discuss painful feelings would always lead to his curling up on the couch with a faraway look in his eyes—and he would be gone. As often as not, these periods were accompanied by Peter jumping off the couch (fairly difficult to do), prowling around the office on all fours and then leaping back onto the couch (extremely difficult to do). The imitation was so flawlessly done, the leaping and prowling so seamless an imitation, that it required only a very brief suspension of belief in reality to see him as he saw himself.

I soon began to ask Peter what was happening where he was. Then he would describe, in the most vivid details, his actions amid the fauna and flora of the region. As mentioned earlier, his knowledge of details was excellent and correct. Later, when Peter drifted off and we were talking in this way, I asked him what I was, and he replied, "You're a bob-tailed shrew." Further scurrying in the library revealed that a bob-tailed shrew was a rather small animal, one that a snow leopard could easily kill with a swipe of his paw. The delusion was complete. Now Peter not only was master in his own land but had made me the frightened little animal in his world that he was in mine.

That first summer arrived too soon for me. Peter and I had only been seeing each other for three months but I already looked forward to each session. They were sometimes difficult and frustrating, and sometimes I had trouble staying in touch with the details of his fantasy; yet it was a privilege to be with him. I began to see another way in which his choice of an almost extinct animal was appropriate; Peter himself was a very special boy.

Just before the summer Peter saw "Star Wars." He was totally captivated by this film and described it in great detail to me at his last session. He said, "You must see it," and I assured him that I would. Often when a patient tells you that you must read a book or see a movie, the book or movie says something particular to him. So I went to see "Star Wars"; I was enchanted by it and pleased because in this fantasy Peter was identifying with a human hero. A few weeks later I saw "Star Wars" T-shirts for sale and bought one with Peter's name on it. I sent it to him with a note. It is important to show patients that you have listened and followed through; for Peter, who felt that no one was listening, it was especially important.

Peter's mother and stepfather came to see me once during that first summer while he was away. His mother wanted to know if I had been able to determine whether or not Peter was homosexual. I felt it was vital that they know how troubled Peter was without violating his confidence. He had told me that I was the only one who knew of his other world; he had sworn me to secrecy. At the same time it was necessary to defuse the sexual issue. In spite of having expressed the desire to be a girl, Peter was probably less consciously interested in sex than most twelve year olds. So I replied that the question of Peter's sexuality would perhaps be an interesting one if Peter ever decided to be a person.

Peter's stepfather's mouth dropped open. "Are you talking about psychosis?"

I said no, but told them that Peter spent most of his time living in a fantasy world, the details of which had to remain confidential. His mother asked how it was possible that they had not known; how had he managed at school?

I asked what the school had been reporting these last three years. She said that the school felt Peter was bright but always daydreaming; he was definitely not working up to potential. It seemed clear, then, that Peter could not work up to potential because he spent so much time in his fantasy world.

When Peter returned from his father's, he seemed genuinely happy to be back. After previous visits he had usually been in an angry and aggressive mood. He soon filled me in on the details of his summer, and it seemed clear that he felt uncomfortable with his father but was establishing a good rapport with his stepmother.

Peter had complained about his stepfather in the months preceding the summer break; he found him demanding (of Peter's services) and prone to favoritism with his own two sons. Now I was beginning to detect a similar dissatisfaction with his real father. When I said that this seemed so and asked him why, he gave me what struck me as a rational (but untruthful) explanation concentrating on feeling uncomfortable talking with his father. It was easier talking to his stepmother because she "understood." When I pursued this, Peter disappeared. It was a shock. One minute he had been happy and bubbly and now the faraway glaze came into his eyes. At the beginning of the hour I had forgotten his fragility. Now he was giving me the clearest of reminders.

Unlike other times, however, when he had moved around and I was able to communicate with him, now questioning was useless. He had just curled up and seemed adrift in his own world. After a while I stopped talking to him and just sat and watched him on the couch, first, looking carefully to see if he would give me any clue as to how to get in, and second, letting myself feel my own feelings.

My own feelings said, "Go over and be close to him." If I hesitated it was only to consider whether it was his need I was sensing or my own need to "do something." I decided it was both and got up and sat down next to him on the couch. He snarled, backed up and bared his fangs. I moved back a little and then, cautiously, reached out my hand to touch his arm. His arm did not move, but his skin did. Slowly I stroked his arm, little by little moving closer, until finally I was able to stroke the hair on his head. And so we stayed until the end of the session.

Peter's complaints about his stepfather also concerned one other area, Peter's drawings. Peter, it seemed, was fascinated with female gymnasts and Wonder Woman, and these were what he primarily drew. His stepfather considered the activity "faggish" (so apparently did his mother) and did not hesitate to tell Peter so. So he had submerged his drawing; he did less and less of it (his father had fretted over this decline in artistic activity in one part of a long letter to me), and what he did do was often done as a clandestine activity.

Offhand it seemed likely that Peter was looking, in the grace and strength of the female athlete (and in Wonder

Woman with her magical transformation), for a human equivalent of his strength and grace as a snow leopard. Again he was searching for a human identification. It was being endangered by the attitude of his parents so I set out to counter that. "Draw for me," I suggested. And so he began to. The first drawings were rigid (see Figure 1) and the bodies sometimes were not clearly male or female (although he usually said they were female).

I felt they were quite good for a youngster his age and told him so. Peter's drawings of females improved over time (as did his drawings of males) and came to include aspects that in retrospect I could see in a more primitive form in his athlete and Wonder Woman drawings, but which I had not anticipated. The females became extremely powerful, both in body and in magical powers. The phallic symbolism of these magical powers was visually obvious in the drawings (see Figures 2 and 3). Force fields emanating from the head and power bursts from the hands emerged.

Later, I was able to feel how powerful he believed his mother (all women?) to be. He sought not only identification but also representation in the drawings. And yet his ambivalence about women possessing such power seemed obvious in the names that he often gave them, for example, DARK-LIGHT (?! evil and good fused together) for Figure 2, or SAPHIRE (another "dark light") for one of his other female drawings (see Figure 4). In stark contrast, a male figure drawn at the same time as Figures 2 and 3 (Figure 5) is rather static and impotent-looking. However, my interpretations of these drawings ("This woman looks so powerful," etc.) were met with no comment and so, obviously, were too early, if correct.

Figure 1

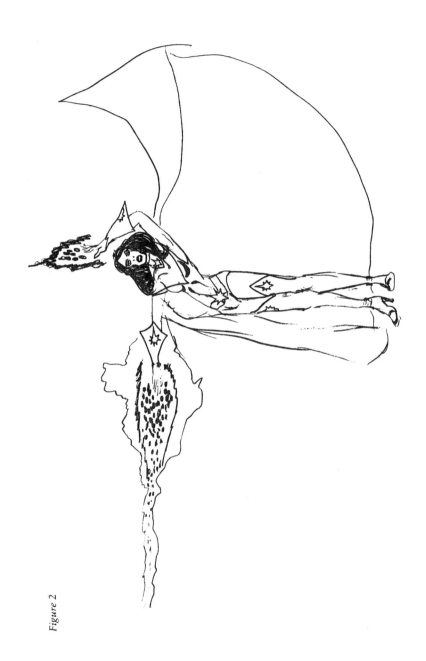

Figure 2

Figure 3

Figure 4

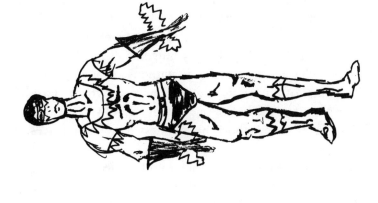

Figure 5

In the meantime, the new school year was about half over. Peter seemed to be spending more time with a group of boys in his grade (remember they were generally one year his junior) involved in fantasy games where they pretended that they were animals and natives in the jungle. Unfortunately, Peter rarely saw any of these boys after school. At home, of course, he had no trouble involving his much younger half-brothers in similar fantasy games, but with them he pretended he was a mouse. Perhaps, in doing so he was protecting them from his rage toward them and from the strength with which it might surface if he expressed it as the leopard. He had already seen, in the accidental breaking of his younger half-brother's collarbone, what harm he could do with just a shove.

Most of our sessions continued along the pattern laid out almost at the beginning of that school year. As long as I let Peter go on about his painless daily experiences, he remained happy and verbal. He did, little by little, fill in the details of his life with his two families, his jealousies, his disappointments, his hopes. But I was not allowed to broach any painful area. He would withdraw, allowing me only to be physically near him and to stroke him. I began to tell him, as soon as he would go off, "Peter, you are going away to the Himalayas because what I said is painful to you"; I hoped that, with time, he would become comfortable with the idea and with the knowledge that I knew why he was going off.

Christmas came and Peter was off again. Following up on many discussions of his unrelatedness to time, I sent Peter a watch for Christmas, my way of saying, "Now you can be oriented to time." It went over well; Peter came back very happy and on time to his first session, wearing the watch proudly.

In the sessions I continued to make my interpretations when Peter would go off to the Himalayas. I became more insistent, repeating the interpretation many times, in many ways, before remaining silent and joining Peter on his mountain. And each time I wondered, "How long can I keep this up today? How far can I go? How fragile is he still? Please don't let me hurt him." My feeling for his feelings had intensified many times over the year. We had become intimates, but not in the real world as much as in his delusion. In his world he could kill me with a casual swipe of his paw; in my world he was my delicate, hurting little boy. I knew there were traumas in his early childhood. I knew he would have to face them, acknowledge his loss, his pain. And yet I felt the time was not right. I felt he didn't trust me enough in my world. Feeling the intensity of his pain, I could not bring *myself* to make him face it. The physical intimacy of the many sessions made me feel protective of him (finally, overprotective?); the intimacy we achieved in the detailed beauty of his quiet and harmonious life in the delusion made me hesitate to be the agent of its destruction.

In retrospect I know I was overcautious because of the countertransference feelings Peter invoked in me. At the time I considered this issue many times but refused to see it fully. I rationalized away my overprotectiveness. Besides, his delusion was beautiful and what did I have to offer him in exchange? A world that had already hurt him in the most terrible ways and that would eventually, probably, hurt him again. Then I would argue the other point of view with myself. Of course he would be hurt in the real world. We are all hurt. Vulnerability is the price we pay for relationships that have depth. In his delusion he was safe and could not get hurt, but neither could any of his relationships in the real world be anything but superficial. The only intimate relationship he had was with me, and only because I was careful not to hurt and because I went into the delusion. Clearly that was no good for him either. I debated and time went by.

Peter turned thirteen and spring vacation came. When he came back we began, somewhat tentatively, to discuss his gender and sexual preference. The court papers filed by various psychiatrists, court counselors, and so on, during the custody battle were full of concern, on the part of Peter's mother, that it be determined if he were prehomosexual (?!) and extremely effeminate. The negative attitudes that he had lived with regarding his effeminacy made the whole issue extremely sensitive. I wanted Peter to know that he was fine just the way he was and that whatever sexual orientation developed would be normal if it were truly him. He seemed indifferent. When we talked about his gender preference Peter said that he felt now that he would rather be a boy, and added, almost parenthetically, that his Dad had had a similar problem. When I asked him, Peter said that last spring, after he confided his gender confusion to his father, his father had told him that he understood, since he himself had had similar feelings at Peter's age and was, in fact, a bisexual. Peter had said nothing but had felt enormous rage surge up toward his father. For years he had believed that his parents' divorce had been his mother's fault exclusively. She had abandoned him and his Dad. Now, suddenly, it was as if, in not telling him about his bisexuality, his father had conspired to keep him hating his mother while not hating him. Suddenly, he hated his father. He hated his stepfather. All the feelings of many years had suddenly become a lie. And then the delusion of the snow leopard began to form in his mind.[2]

In the real world Peter was a frightened little mouse, terrified by unpredictable adults and his own murderous rage. In the mountains of his delusion the rage found an outlet—as the snow leopard he killed and so the rage was spent. Years later this theme emerged quite clearly in a sublimated form as a short story Peter submitted to school (see appendix). There the themes of madness, controlling adults, delusions, rage and murder all converge. The rage is satisfied in the real world through murder and destruction (a holocaust—a totally consuming fire offering to the godless skies), but then peace only comes with madness.

No wonder, then, the retreat to the delusion when I brought up painful material. It was not only to protect

---

[2] Those clinicians who are drawn to genetic explanations will, I think, find the following (a very short part of a letter from Peter's father) interesting:

> . . . my family has a history of mental illness not unlike the kind you outlined to me in Peter's case. My father's mother sat in front of a wood stove in a tenement . . . from the time I remember her first at the age of five until her death a few years ago, distant, somewhere else, uncommunicative, but not violent or destructive. Where she was as she sat there neither I nor my parents even knew, although we knew it was a response to her wretched life. My aunt, my father's sister, was committed to [a] State Hospital when I was a teenager and is still there, suffering, as I've been told, from some dementia. My father too has for years spaced out somewhere else. . . .

himself but to protect me from the rage he felt toward me for hurting him. No wonder, then, that he let me stroke him and hold him. It quieted his anger, made me a love object again, made it safe to come back to the real world.

Peter's anger at the world and his ambivalence appeared in sublimated form in his poetry of that time. On one hand he was ready to give up the delusion, to scream out his hatred to the world, to destroy the old and emerge from his own ashes (the holocaust again, this time leading to rebirth). Fittingly he saw this in the symbol of the phoenix, which appeared at this time and remained his special private symbol (see Figure 6, p. 39) for a number of years.

PHOENIX

I who have broken the bonds
of my self constricting immaturity
hereby declare an everlasting
Peace to my every whim.
Hear me world I
Am The One
needed least in
your evolutionary
functions. I am
no longer the blob of
plasma known by others
for I am
PHOENIX

On the other hand, he was terrified of what such a change might mean. He was afraid of his own anger and aggression and so saw it all around him. And he was afraid that it would kill him and hoped, therefore, for the person he most wanted to hold and comfort him, the person who originally abandoned him, his mother.

The Snow Leopard

Mommy Hold Me for I Fear I am Dying

Why must the Earth end so suddenly?
I've only begun to live.
Why is it that I see omnipotent explosions of red and yellow?
I fear all that is around me,
and all I see is endless masses of green and yellow flowers.
I know not why the earth and sky are crumbling all around me.
I know not why the Heavens fall to the feet of my oppressor.
Why must the earth be so aggressive?
Why must we prove our strength and power?
It hurts me deeply to see my fellow man
squander and slave in an endless quest for power.
Why must the earth be so aggressive?
Why must all men and women try so hard
to gain unneeded supremacy?
Mommy hold me for I fear I am Dying.
Mommy save me
for my soul is lost in the endless mists of time.
Mommy hold me
the sorrows of a million tears are gone.
Mommy do not cradle my self pity
for there cannot be happiness for all.
Mommy hold me
for I need no longer worry for myself.
Mommy the earth has no mercy
but is as cruel as a lion pouncing on its prey.

All of Peter's life began to fall together in my mind. I felt that I knew now where I had to go, what I had to do. Peter himself gave me the go-ahead signal. In our last session before the summer, he said, "It's hard to live there [in the world of the snow leopard]—it's lonely and cold." Peter was getting ready to give up the delusion.

That summer went very rapidly for me. Peter was back almost before I really began to feel his absence. He rushed in at his first session and hugged me. He was much bigger now than a year and a half ago, although still a head shorter than I. He no longer had his androgynous twelve-year-old body. He was an early teen and clearly all boy. He had had a good summer and was looking forward to seeing his school friends again. The specter of school itself was another matter. Peter, despite what was emerging as a genuinely superior intellect, continued to do poorly in school. In part it was lack of faith in himself. He couldn't believe me when I told him how smart he was.

That fall, as the sessions continued, Peter became noticeably nervous. He hid more often in the caves and shadows of his delusion, and work along the lines we had started in the spring did not progress. I knew where I wanted to go, but, in retrospect, I see that I was probably afraid. Was Peter afraid, too? Did he remember his parting complaint about the coldness and loneliness? He would have to risk everything to give up his private world; he would have to expose himself all over again with nothing but me to protect him, with no one but me to run to. The terror must have been enormous and growing each day as the healthy part of Peter moved toward the break with the delusion and rejoining with the real world.

And then, one Friday evening, Peter's mother called to say that he was threatening to kill himself by jumping out the window. He was, in fact, on the windowsill, many floors above the street. I held on while she relayed my messages to Peter and finally he came in so that I could speak with him. I promised I would drive right over to see him, insisting all the while that he must not give in to this impulse to destroy himself just when he was so close to helping himself. I got his mother back on the phone and told her not to take her eyes off him until I got there. And so she sat there, holding her son while he cried and cried, saying only, over and over, "The white leopard. The white leopard."

In the next few sessions I pushed Peter very hard. There was no more time for protectiveness or, I realized, for possessiveness. I confronted him over and over with the by now well-known facts of his life and his anger over them. I urged him to see how he hid from his rage out of his fear that it would destroy him and the objects of his love/hatred. Each time I would only get so far, and then he would escape.

I came to see my stroking him as negative. He was terrified of his rage; by my actions, I was saying quite clearly that I was frightened, too. Peter probably felt that I was afraid for myself, when, in fact, I was afraid for him. But I had fear and he knew it.

I decided to pull back. I decided not to go into the delusion anymore to force Peter out. And so it was that when he again escaped, curled up in his corner of the couch, I moved to the opposite side on the couch and said, "Peter, you're very angry with me, and it's very important that you come back to this office and know that you are here and it's me that you are angry with." I repeated it over and over, looking into eyes that did not see me. I became insistent, demanding, and deliberately goaded him. I told him over and over that I would not come in today, that he must come back. I told him over and over that he was angry with me and that he needed to face and express that anger. I told him I knew he feared his anger, but I assured him that his anger would not hurt me, or himself. I pushed him and pushed him; then, without warning, he leaped on me.

He did not leap as a person but as a leopard, his claws extended, his fangs bared. He was smaller than me but the impact knocked us both off the couch and onto the floor. Then he really went after me. He had a decided advantage for a while; he was on top of me and had the strength well known in psychotic episodes. But I was stronger and larger and eventually I got on top of him and pinned his arms so that he could no longer claw me.

His eyes were shut tight, as if to open them would admit the real world and everything I had been pushing him to do. Feeling this, I insisted that I would not let him up until he opened his eyes and I was convinced that he realized that he was in my office and that he was angry with me. He thrashed about for a few more minutes while I repeated my terms. Finally, he calmed down and opened his eyes, and as he did so he burst into tears. I immediately relaxed my hold on him, and he ran to the couch and cried and cried.

I went over to him and held him tight while he sobbed. I stroked his hair and kissed the top of his head. Finally he was quiet. He held me and I held him. And I asked him if he liked this, being held and comforted, and he said, "Yes." And so I said, "Then there is something I must tell you. In the world of the snow leopard you are the king, but you are all alone. The warmth of human comfort exists only in this world."

And it was evening, and it was morning, the first day.

Christmas came and went. Peter was going to be fourteen. Our sessions had changed dramatically. The snow leopard was gone. Peter's need (ability?) to withdraw into the delusion decreased or his ability (need?) to believe in it did. And our relationship changed drastically, also. I was no longer his animal companion in delusion, but we were still as fused psychologically as ever. Just as I had been a major element in completing his delusional world, so now I was a major element in completing his real world.

Having left the security and isolation of his delusion, Peter now had to rely heavily on me as a secure model in the real world. As he had counted on me not to hurt him in his world, now he counted on me not to hurt him in this one. Since he had been badly traumatized before and had trusted me to love him, now a full-blown "perfect mother" transference developed. I would be the perfect mother who would love him and not abandon him. I would be omnipresent and all-knowing.

On the emotional level I felt comfortable enough with Peter's demands and expectations. But in all other respects this transference made me terribly uncomfortable. Peter needed to make me perfect so my stability would be assured. But in doing so he needed to feel that everything I did and everything about me was also perfect. Although there was a partially good side to the transference, it was also, in its own way, neurotic and destructive. My discomfort, I realized, came from the realization that eventually I would "fail" to be perfect, just as his mother (and father, too), his original perfect objects, had failed. What would happen then?

As it is essential to interpret, over and over again, the dynamic at work in a negative transference, it became essential here, too, to interpret the dynamic underlying this (on the surface) positive one. My initial attempts were met with hysterically angry fits on Peter's part. Any suggestion that I was not perfect in some way would set Peter off. He would become enraged, saying, "That's not true. You're just saying that so that I won't think you're perfect, but I know that you're perfect." He would keep it up, becoming increasingly agitated and often crying. Often I gave up even attempting any rebuttal. The time was certainly not right. It seemed better to use my "perfect" state to influence Peter in his increasingly strong social and familial strivings.

Another aspect of this "perfect mother" period was that Peter automatically assumed that anything that went wrong between us was his fault. He constantly apologized for everything—so constantly, in fact, that it almost reached the point where he would say "I'm sorry" as he walked into the office. I made this habit even more ridiculous by mentioning it often, for instance, pointing out when he hadn't said "I'm sorry" for at least five minutes. It soon became a joke between us; nevertheless, although its irrational basis was clear to him, this habit of the transference did not stop.

Peter's relationships at home began to improve. He started taking piano lessons. He spent more time away from home with friends. He was still not doing as well at school as I would have expected and, indeed, was threatened with the prospect of summer school. Peter's mother called to say that according to the custody agreement Peter would be allowed to live for one year during his adolescence with his father; she wanted me to discuss this with Peter and form my own opinion about whether this would be a good thing for Peter.

So Peter and I began to talk about a move to his father's home, with his father, stepmother, and two-year-old half-brother. Although Peter's relationship with his father had improved over the Christmas and spring vacations that year, he still talked about the move with tremendous ambivalence. He still felt very uncomfortable with his father but could not put his finger on the reason why.

At the same time Peter's emerging sexual interests became a topic of therapy, and his intense ambivalence about homosexuality emerged. On the one hand Peter did not want to know what homosexuals did together, but on the other hand he did. It was both repulsive and exciting, energizing the dynamics of his very early childhood cross-dressing and effeminacy.[3] In fact, he confided that often, when I had held and stroked him and he had been in the real world, he pretended that he was a girl and I his lover.

It seemed clear, then, that his discomfort with his father was acutely related to this issue. Eventually it became clear that, in spite of his improving relationship with his father, Peter felt that no matter how his father loved him,

---

[3]The following is an excerpt from the psychiatric evaluation done at the time of the custody battle:

> . . . Peter [had] difficulty understanding his mother's behavior and . . . [came] to feel that there must be something about him that she doesn't like. Being intelligent, he also [knew] that it [was] really his father that she [wanted] to leave.
>
> . . . In order to make sure his mother wouldn't abandon him, Peter had to be unlike his father. To a young boy this would mean primarily not being a boy. So for some time Peter tested whether being a girl would be more acceptable to his mother.

he would never love him as he had loved other men. The discomfort settled on this buried dynamic—the simultaneous attraction and repulsion created by this unconscious wish for homosexual incest. In our physical closeness Peter had been acting out this wish with his perfect, all-accepting transference father, first as a girl, and then, later, as the boy he had become.

It became clear to me that, difficult as it would probably be, Peter needed to live with his father. But the idea of doing it for one year was all wrong. It made no sense to pull Peter out of his school in one city, put him in a new school for his first year of high school, an often difficult transition point in adolescence, and then try to transplant him back in tenth grade. Also, I doubted whether Peter could really get to know his father in one year, and clearly he needed to find out for himself who this man really was—it was now or never, really. Who knew where Peter would go after high school?

So I suggested, first to Peter, and then to his mother, that he go to live with his father for the entire four years of high school.

The month preceding the summer break was a difficult and frustrating one for Peter. In sessions we were still locking horns over my "perfectness"; out of sessions I was fighting with Peter's school, which had requested that he stay for the first six weeks of summer for summer school. Eventually I worked my way up to the headmaster and explained that Peter's need to be with his father was greater than any other need; I suggested that the father's offer of individual tutors for Peter over the summer appeared more than adequate. But the school insisted that unless Peter went to their summer school they could never be sure that Peter had covered their curriculum. No amount of reasoning did any good, and at our next session I had to tell Peter that I had failed (how reality comes to our aid!) to persuade the school to let him go. I had finally failed Peter—how relieving it was and for Peter not so destructive as his unconscious had imagined. After all, I was on his side and wanted him to be with his father; I had lost in my battle with an uncaring establishment. So I remained the one who loved him wholly, but at the same time I became defeatable, less than perfect, human.

In the next few sessions I helped Peter put this realization into words. I discussed his new summer plans, expressed my anger at his school and its headmaster, as well as my regret at my impotence, and did everything possible to fix his disillusionment on the real events so that it would be more difficult to deny if he tried to do so in the future. Then, having made a good case for the negative aspects of the situation, I turned to what positive aspects there might be. And so Peter coped with his first major disappointment since his return to reality.

I put our extra time together to one additional good purpose. Since Peter was using summer school, in part, as a demonstration of how dumb he was, I countered that we now had the time to settle the question once and for all. We set aside time for me to administer the Wechsler Intelligence Scale for Children to Peter. Peter really believed in me by this time and, I think, was genuinely convinced by the results. In school-related areas he was performing at average or better levels for his age. But in those areas generally acknowledged as most highly correlated with genuine cognitive capacity, his intellectual functioning was genuinely superior. [4]

The summer visit to his father, then, was really very short. When Peter returned everyone seemed to have agreed that he would live with his father and complete high school at one school. It meant that this would be the last year of therapy.

Peter's eighth grade year was, especially compared with his previous four years, a triumph. Suddenly no longer stupid, he seemed able to grasp abstract ideas and formulate deep personal thoughts. His drawing progressed, and a budding interest in drama led to his involvement in the annual school musical production. He began to go to more concerts and theater productions and shared with me his enthusiastic reviews and imitations. His piano lessons continued and his appreciation for music deepened. Trained since early childhood as a pianist myself, I traded many thoughts with Peter on piano playing, eventually, by the spring of that last year, sharing practice tapes with him.

In school Peter really began to blossom. His friendships deepened as he progressed from his earlier game playing to intensely felt personal relationships. He had

[4]Those clinicians familiar with the scoring of the WISC will, I hope, agree that this statement is adequately supported by scaled scores of 20 (!) in Similarities, 16 in Block Design, 16 in Object Assembly, and 13 in Comprehension. Also, Peter's scaled score of 16 in Digit Span was the result of success on seven digits forward and eight backward, a type of performance often associated with a child whose intellect rises to the challenge of the more difficult task.

friends of both sexes, but no girlfriend or boyfriend. Aware of the origins of his troubled mind, Peter was kind, understanding, sensitive, and perhaps above all, gracious in his relations with others.

Bettelheim says:

> To characterize the function of the analyst—someone who could greatly facilitate the emergence of a new personality, making the process of the change a safe one—Freud often used the simile of the midwife. As the midwife neither creates the child nor decides what he will be but only helps the mother to give birth to him safely, so the psychoanalyst can neither bring the new personality into being nor determine what it ought to be. . . . The poet H. D. (Hilda Doolittle), speaking of her experience with Freud during her analysis, said, "He is midwife to the soul."[5]

I felt more like a lucky gardener coming across a beautifully laid out garden with the flower bulbs planted upside down. I turned them right side up so as to grow out toward the world, patted the soil, fed them, watered them. And they grew and blossomed. But I, like the gardener, did not make the flowers, nor did I lay out the arrangement. Peter's true personality was uniquely his own.

As the year progressed sublimation took other forms in Peter. He began to cook seriously, taking on as a thoroughly enjoyed duty the preparation of dinner for his mother, stepfather, and half-brothers at least once a week. On a number of occasions he arrived at sessions with pies still warm from the oven. For his birthday that year he asked for, and I bought him, a good copper mixing bowl.

[5]Bettelheim, Bruno. *Freud and Man's Soul.* New York: Random House, 1983, p. 36.

And the snow leopard delusion took on sublimated form as an ability to do multiple animal imitations for his friends. His subtlety in these was so good that he could do, for instance, several different types of easily distinguishable dogs.

And so the fall came and went. Christmas vacation came and Peter went off to his father's home. In a few weeks he was back. His birthday came and went. Spring was approaching and as I began seriously to consider Peter's leaving therapy I felt a terrible sadness. Just as Peter had seen me, in the transference, as perfect mother and father, I now realized that, in my countertransference, he had become beloved son. Of course if analysis is a "cure . . . effected by love"[6] then such a transference-countertransference is not only inevitable but quintessentially human. How can we really help if we do not love and are not loved? In our last months together I knew that if I called Peter's mother and told her that living with his father would be harmful to him she never would have allowed him to go. My anguish came from contemplating, even fantasizing, doing this, while in another part of my mind knowing that I would never do it. I knew my sadness for what it was on that most truly human level, the sacrificial one, where I knew that I would lose Peter.

Often, in clinical summaries, little reference is made to the countertransference. Everyone writes that analytic

[6]McGuire, William (Ed.); Manheim, Ralph and Hull, R. F. C. (Trans.). *The Freud/Jung Letters: The Correspondence between Sigmund Freud and C. G. Jung.* Princeton: Princeton University Press, 1974. Letter 8F, pp. 12–13.

progress is dependent on the emergence of a recognizable and analyzable transference, that is, one that can be interpreted and worked through. But if this is so, then so must countertransference be inevitable. Perhaps we avoid mentioning it in the literature because doing so gives us the secure, if false, feeling that we, the analysts, are different from our patients. And yet, although in terms of insight and understanding we often are different, in this most human arena we are not—and we must not ever delude ourselves into thinking we are. On this most fundamental level we and our patients are equals; the bond between patient and analyst is based on our common humanity; pain and suffering, loneliness, the human condition are our common glue. If an analyst is perfect, he can be of no use to others. If I do not also know of pain, how can I feel yours, how can I truly understand what you are talking about?

The trouble with countertransference arises then, I think, only when the patient's pain touches our own in a very fundamental place and we cannot bring ourselves to make our patients face this pain, both out of misguided protectiveness and as a way of avoiding facing it ourselves. While I agonized over my anticipated personal loss of Peter, I knew that time was running out and Peter had not yet worked through the most fundamental trauma of his life, his mother's abandonment. And yet, I could not get beyond myself on the subject of this trauma. Discussions of this event remained intellectual and contained nothing of the energetic emotionality that had emerged around other issues.

I knew I was at fault; unconsciously I was obviously leading the sessions into digressions when things threatened to go beyond the didactic. And I knew why.[7] Knowing this pain of emotional abandonment, I could not bring Peter fully face to face with the trauma of his own more serious and real abandonment.

I was still struggling to overcome this difficulty in myself, as I knew I must, when reality, that most spontaneous of therapists, came to my aid once again. Peter's relationship with one of his friends who was a girl grew into a boy-friend-girlfriend one. It was almost summer and Peter had had a very good year. The advent of a girlfriend and two upcoming dates for summer operas in the park seemed a fitting climax.

In retrospect I do not know what precipitated the next events—whether it was having a girlfriend, which awakened deep-seated fears of being abandoned by a woman after loving her, or simply an unconscious reaching to resolution. Peter showed up for the last hour of my day. He seemed happy and was lying on the couch facing me and talking about his anticipated dates. Suddenly he was not talking; he had stopped in mid-sentence. At first I thought he was just reaching for the right word or thought and I

[7]In my own analysis one constant theme was "a child is dying," but, although the effects of this theme and my fear appeared often enough in real life, its origin defied elucidation for three years. Then, out of curiosity I asked my mother about an often repeated story that she had, for medical reasons, left me for a week or so after my birth. She said that this had seemed to have very little effect, but that she had become severely depressed after my birth and had, in fact, on many occasions during my first year, been *unable to bring herself to touch me*. So the child who was dying was me. Facing this realization fully was the most painful event of my many years of analytic work.

said nothing. As he continued to seem off in his own thoughts, I said, "And then what?" but he did not seem to hear me.

I became alarmed and called out, "Peter, Peter." I went over to the couch because I thought he had fainted. But, although his breathing was shallow, his eyes were wide open. It had been over a year and a half since he had disappeared like this, over a year and a half since the last session of the delusion, and I was shocked to realize that it could suddenly reappear like this, with no warning. I went back to my chair and tried to reach him on a verbal, if emotional, level. "Peter," I asked, "what is wrong? Where are you? Please let me in."

But he remained silent and motionless. I was in agony, imagining that all the gains of three years of work had suddenly been erased in this recapitulation of symptoms.

After a long while Peter suddenly rose and leaped off the couch. The snow leopard was back, and because of Peter's much larger size, more awesome and disturbing than ever. Peter began to prowl around the office. My attempts to reach him in the delusion were all useless. He bumped into things; chairs fell over; books came falling off their shelves. The leopard was enraged and the power that Peter now had was frighteningly apparent in the destruction he was causing.

Then he loped into a corner between one of the bookcases and the door and turned around and around like an animal in the corner of a cage. Finally he sat down and raising one paw, claws (nails) extended, drew it across his face in an obvious effort to claw his face off. By the time I yelled, "No, Peter, no," he had scratched himself and pulled out some of his hair.

I was on him in a few steps. I yelled, "Peter, I will not allow you to destroy yourself," and grabbed his hands. But he was much bigger and stronger now. He tossed me aside quite easily and reached for his face and hair again. His eyes were shut tight, a reminder of that much earlier session. But that time he had tried to destroy me; this time he was trying to destroy himself. I grabbed him again and we began to wrestle. He did nothing that could possibly have hurt me; he spent only enough time with me to get his hands free so he could get at himself.

I was fortunate to be able to pin his arms with my knees and his wrists with my hands. I was exhausted, and, I think, so was he. I looked down on him, my hurt little boy, my beloved son; he was crying and his lips were moving though I could not make out the words. I said, "What?" and then bent down so my ear was over his mouth.

And I heard in a five-year-old voice, his memory no doubt of his own five-year-old voice, a little boy I had never known crying out, between his sobs, "Mommy, mommy, please come back. I'll be good."

It hit me like an arrow in the heart, and I burst into tears. "Oh God, Peter," I said, "it wasn't your fault. You were just a little boy." And then suddenly his big fifteen-year-old voice came back and he screamed, "They never wanted me," and pushed me off him with one immense shove. He rose on his knees, still crying, and I grabbed him and held him. He went soft in my arms and I relaxed, sitting down on the floor, his head in my lap. When he stopped crying he looked up at me and said, "You're the only person who ever hugged me."

And it was evening, and it was morning, the second day.

During the next few sessions Peter and I spent our time trying to understand and work through the recapitulation-of-symptoms session. Then we turned back to the real world and spent two wonderful sessions listening to the music and discussing the stories of the operas he was going to hear with his girlfriend (Rigoletto and Madame Butterfly). He had his dates, lying contentedly and romantically under the stars, even kissing his date.

And then he was off, spending the summer with his mother and half-brothers as he would be leaving them in the fall. I saw him once more and took a few photographs of him as we left my office. Then he was off to live with his father.

As if in recognition of his belatedly discovered brilliance, his new school skipped him out of ninth grade and into tenth. He became involved in a whirlwind schedule of school, dance classes, drama, choir singing, piano lessons, and parties with friends.

He wrote excitedly of his busy new life, and I was happy. Once, in November, he was at a party and saw a plant which closely resembled one that had been in his parents' home when he was five; he had begun to imagine that he was there again and five again and had burst into tears. He called me, appropriately anxious as to whether he would always have to fear "slipping back." He calmed down and the incident was resolved.

I saw Peter at Christmastime and later again the next

summer. He was full of enthusiasm about everything. His choir singing had led to his being chosen for a small chamber group that toured together. His involvement in drama had led to his auditioning and getting a part in the following year's musical production; his dancing had changed his once soft, young adolescent body into a more muscled one of which he was proud. He had fallen in love with early classical vocal music and was something of an expert, explaining it in detail—and so teaching me.

Moreover, he had fallen in love with a girl and his sexual yearnings were reaching maturity. He continued, as before, sensitive, kind, and gracious.

In the complex sea of our personalities, perhaps, there are many islands of functioning. On some are our fantasies, on some our realities, on some our dreams or our delusions. For Peter, his private island of delusion was now one on which he had very little time to spend. And although the snow leopard will always be there, Peter will not. Or so I hope and pray.

As I sat in my chair in my office, reading through this paper, I looked up and realized for the first time that on the bookshelf directly behind me (how subtle is the unconscious!) is my crystal Lalique (hence, milky white) sculpture of a leopard. And directly across from it, in front of me, is my photograph of Peter at fifteen, happy and alive, smiling at me across the unfathomable void.

APPENDIX

Figure 6

IN APPRAISAL OF THE MOCKINGBIRD

Light. Its appearance was hailed by the calling of the mockingbird. The mockingbird had a nice sound, a warm sound, the kind of sound that makes you happy to be alive. The sun started to rise. It spread its wings and flew into the heavens, like a phoenix from its ashes. The light had cascaded rapturously across the olive groves and our endless fields of wheat. I could see the wheat blowing harmoniously in the morning breeze. The world was alive once more.

I liked watching the sun rise. It made me feel like I was a part of nature. The rising of the sun . . .

"Wake up! Wake up! The sun is shining in the sky. Rise and shine and wipe your eye. . . . "

I had to make my bed every day. I'd spread my over-sized green quilt over an almost grotesquely large brass bed. I felt dwarfed by it. I hated my room. The ceiling must have been at least twenty feet high. The beams that ran across the ceiling were covered with cob-webs. My room had the smallest fireplace. It was covered in green and black tiles.

You see what they did, giving me this room. It's not fair! They always did this to me.

I sometimes wondered why I allowed them to let the house fall apart. Of course I had had very little say in this matter. But after they . . . they . . . well then I could yell all I liked and they wouldn't bother me. This house was so dingy. Why couldn't more light shine in? I remember when it was dark, mother sang me to sleep;

"Hush little baby don't say a word, momma's gonna buy you a mockingbird. If that mockingbird don't sing momma's gonna buy you a diamond ring . . . "

Momma never bought me a mockingbird or a diamond ring. She must have lied to me.

Why was the kitchen so empty? Nothing was in the pantry but a can of soup and some bread crusts. It was my birthday and nothing was in the kitchen. I was going to have a nice dinner all by myself, but I couldn't. Dinner . . .

"Sit up straight!"

"Don't pick at your food!"

. . . "I will." . . . "I won't." . . .

They had been so pushy. I wonder why I had allowed them to live . . . to be around as long as I had. After they were gone, I thought I could eat any way I wanted. But there was nothing to eat.

The light had beamed in through the open door. Opening the front door had been a good idea. It shone into the formal parlor and danced on the crystal chandelier. It reflected off the lamp and had played havoc with the colours of the china figures. I didn't like the china figures. They were my grandmother's favorites, but I didn't like them. The one in the middle, the red and green soldier, he was the one that I hated the most. He had always lurked in the shadow shrouded corner as I had walked by. He had waited there every night, ready to pounce on me. That's why one day I had taken a stone and had thrown it at him. After that, he had no head.

When the door bell had rung, I didn't want to answer. I

thought it would be someone to see my parents. My uncle, John, had peered in through the parlor door. I had forgotten that I had left the front door open.

. . . "Hello uncle."

"Are your parents at home?" he had frothed at the mouth as he spoke and his words were full of such spite.

. . . "Yes, but you can't see them."

He proceeded in telling me that he wanted to see them. That it was important. That I should go and get them, and not to be sassy. I don't like him either.

I went to my parents' room and looked at the bed. They were there, sleeping as always. I smiled at them, but they didn't answer, even though my father was looking right at me!

My uncle had seated himself and puffed heartily at his big detestable cigar. He looked around the kitchen with curious bewilderment. He asked me why the kitchen was in the state it was. I didn't answer. He asked me how soon my parents would be down. I didn't answer. He became annoyed and questioned my behavior. I noticed the axe on the counter. He demanded to know why I was being so uncooperative.

"How did that rhyme go?"

He said he knew my parents would be shocked by my behavior.

"Now I remember it."

"Lizzy Bordon took an axe, gave her mother forty whacks. When she saw what she had done, she gave her father forty-one."

He lay on the floor. My uncle wouldn't move. His cigar was across the floor and had caught the garbage on fire. I knew all those empty food containers would cause trouble. But it was strangely beautiful. The flames engulfed the basket, swallowing it hungrily. Then the rest of the garbage caught too. It became a small column of hell, a burning inferno. I thought I should leave.

The parlor was cooler. But it's so dark, and that soldier, that headless soldier is waiting for me in that same corner.

Did someone move? The kitchen was now consumed by flames, which were slowly eating their way out. I saw someone staring straight at me from out of the dark. Oh, the mirror. There were so many mirrors in this house. Everyone was staring at me! Stop it!

The parlor, the dining room, the library. Help! The mirrors wanted to get me. They were going to eat me. The flames were eating the hall and the stairs. The mirrors, they were going to kill me. The mirrors loved Mother Father and my grandmother. They loved my other brother and sisters. This whole house hated me. The flames were eating into the parlor! I had to get out. The window . . .

The wheat fields are cool. I now can see the house crumbling and falling as the flames, like the sun, reach for the heavens. I can hear them all screaming at me. Mother Father, everyone, even the red and green soldier. Here in the wheat fields it's cool. I can breathe. I sit here and watch as my house and family go, all gone . . . all gone. The wind is strange. Blowing the wheat. I hear the mockingbird. Maybe it's flying away from the fire. It's singing to me, calling farewell. The skies are so beautiful, covered by the blanket which is night. Maybe I'll live here forever. I'll sleep out here. So quiet, everything but the roar of the flames and the blowing of the wind. Mother used to sing to me at night, she'd cradle me and sing;

"Go to sleep, go to sleep, go to sleep little baby. When you wake you shall have cake, and all the pretty little horses: Black and Bay, daple and gray. Coach and six white horses . . . "

2

BENJAMIN L.

A Freudian Case

It is sad to have to say that the power to fly gradually left them. At first Nana tied their feet to the bed-posts so that they should not fly away in the night; and one of their diversions by day was to pretend to fall off buses; but by and by they ceased to tug at their bonds in bed, and found that they hurt themselves when they let go of the bus. In time they could not even fly after their hats. Want of practice they called it; but what it really meant was that they no longer believed.

From Peter Pan *by J. M. Barrie*

A child psychoanalyst can really, fully appreciate receiving a child's trust. Parents, of course, are accustomed to having their children's trust, which they freely give, unless they have lost it in some fashion. But the trust a child comes to place in his psychoanalyst is something special—

it is earned. With our most deeply troubled patients such trust requires the ultimate—a leap of faith. For these children coming *to believe* in the possibility that the analyst really cares is a process filled with terror—terror, at every moment, that it may not be true, and the even greater terror that it is true. Benjamin L. was one of these children.

Benjamin was also a Freudian case in the sense that Freud, from his theoretical point of view, would have been able to explain Benjamin's presenting symptomatology, as well as his early life history, quite neatly. That this could be true of a twelve-year-old patient in the late twentieth century should be a warning that the framework of an analysis must fit the child and not the other way around.

Benjamin's struggles within his family and within himself clearly reflected the psychological oedipal drama so central to Freudian theory. For the reader unfamiliar with this story, I hope the following will not do it too much of an injustice:

As retold in the play by Sophocles, the King of Thebes is warned that any son born to him and the Queen will be his murderer. In a vain attempt to prevent this the King orders his son Oedipus to be cut and left to bleed to death (in some versions the King himself cuts Oedipus). Oedipus is discovered and rescued by a shepherd who raises him to adulthood. The inevitable then unfolds.

Oedipus meets a stranger (his father) on the road and kills him in a dispute over which one should get out of the other one's way. Oedipus proceeds to Thebes, saves the city from the curse of the Sphinx, and is proclaimed the new King. He then marries, unknowingly, his mother.

When the truth is finally revealed, the Queen hangs herself, and Oedipus blinds himself with her brooch.

Freud saw in this legend a universal struggle in which a son's wishes to displace his father to have his mother (and his father's power) all to himself create fear that the father will retaliate against him and castrate him, making him a non-man and a non-threat. So, Freud theorized, in families in which the oedipal longings are in some way encouraged (through circumstance or seductiveness) tremendous anxiety might be engendered, leading to serious psychological and developmental difficulties.

Benjamin initially came to me because I had asked his parents if I might see him at least a few times. I had just terminated a brief (several month) therapy with his younger brother, who had been suffering from a mild depression. Information I had gathered indirectly during the brother's therapy suggested that Benjamin might be a youngster in a great deal of trouble. Since that therapeutic intervention had been quite successful, Benjamin's parents agreed to let me see him and had the faith in me to allow him to continue even when the beginning was obviously difficult.

This chapter is primarily about trust (as, I think, are all the others) and about the question of whether, and how much, an analyst should become involved in the reality of his patient. My direct intervention in Benjamin's life, as the reader will see, had a very significant and long-lasting effect. Perhaps, of course, this point of view is an arrogance or a conceit on my part. Perhaps Benjamin, like a river flowing inevitably toward the sea, would have found another way to the same end without me. Perhaps not.

Benjamin at twelve. Short and chubby with brown hair and deep, searching eyes. From the moment he first walked in I could feel the tension—his tension because he was reaching the point where he could no longer hold himself together, and the tension between us as he correctly sensed, and feared, that I would only help to destroy the boy he had become. He was extremely intellectual.[1] He was chubby, he explained, because, "Sports are stupid. I don't see the point in running around trying to put a ball in a hoop." He did not know anything about popular music because it was "boring and unsophisticated." He only listened to classical music. Life consisted of reading and studying (in social isolation); getting straight A's in school (the proof of his intellectual superiority and, therefore, of the correctness of his lifestyle) was his only preoccupation. I challenged his cherished ideals, and he wept. He wept most of the first session, and the second, and the third. I was hurting him so I retreated, meeting him for the next few months on the intellectual level on which he felt comfortable, secure, and unthreatened.

Several months went by in this way, and then Benja-

---

[1]For those clinicians familiar with the Rorschach, at just twelve years old he gave forty-two (!) responses to the cards, including nine blends and sixteen different content categories.

46

min brought in his first dream; over the next four years there were over one hundred more:

> It was in your office, but the office was different. There was some kind of a board meeting going on, an election between you and another analyst. The other analyst had played an analyst in a movie. I voted for you, and the election came out in your favor, eleven to six.

So, he had decided that I was real (not just someone *acting* the part of an analyst) and elected me to be his analyst. I knew I could now go ahead.

Although I was elected Benjamin's psychoanalyst in his dream, I still faced the formidable work of overcoming his neurotic terror of me and winning the genuine trust needed to really help.

I was extremely fortunate to discover, in the fall of Benjamin's second year in analysis, that he had kept a diary spanning almost the entire first five months of therapy. In this diary Benjamin detailed his struggles to come to terms with me, with analysis, and with his neurotic fears. I hope that the reader will find this battle, presented from a teenager's point of view, as enlightening as I did.

Benjamin's diary entries, all dated, often had the form of an entry followed by a "saying of the day," followed by a cartoon. The very first entry has, as part of the saying of the day, the following: " . . . It's better not to be noticed at all than do a stunt and be dead." For Benjamin, with all his self-doubts, it was better to do nothing than to dare to be alive. He wrote, years later, "I became all thought; the world became a mental exercise which I vainly hoped could be manipulated by rationalizations. I was cautious to a fault—there was a reason for avoiding any action on any front and I was a master at inventing such reasons."

Typical of the neurotic, he saw everything in extreme opposites. One day after a session in which we had discussed "[his] depressed feelings about [his] body, sex, [and] parents" (diary entry), he wrote in the entry that he had been thinking about the session, and the saying of the day was: "Death as cold as it is and as different is actually a part of life." After a few more sessions, the saying of the day was: "Disaster strikes when one's life is finally complete." For Benjamin, to whom any action was equal to becoming "alive," any action was predestined to bring on disaster and death. No wonder he could not bring himself to do anything. No wonder that he hid the real boy inside his overweight body, that learning to swim was a terror, calling school friends an impossibility. How treacherous are the defenses in hurting the very person who created them for protection.

It is not just a youngster's trust that must be gained in those first few critical months of therapy. An analyst must see behind the initial resistances, see deep into his patient and feel the shape of the terror with which the neurotic defenses are keeping his patient in thrall. By acknowledging and accepting this fear we can become our patient's ally against it. A month after the earlier diary entries, after a session which Benjamin recorded as involving a discussion of his fantasies, he wrote as the saying of the day: "Not all neurotic people become crazy."[2]

---

[2]Benjamin also related that, reinforcing this fear, his mother had told him that she had heard a man on the radio who said all creative people were neurotic and that she agreed.

This preoccupation with "going crazy" is very common among neurotic patients; with it the defenses threaten their "creator" with the things he fears most if they are abandoned — losing touch with reality, losing control, chaos, death. A diary entry one month later has Benjamin recalling that in his session, "I said I was worried about going crazy."

A week later the cartoon of the day shows me unlocking a door with Benjamin behind it. I am to set *him* free (Figure 1). Two days later I am unraveling a "complicated knot" labeled "me" (i.e., Benjamin) (Figure 2).

Figure 1

And yet I am also the deliverer of painful news. The diary is full of entries saying, "I thought about what Fred said." Two weeks after I am seen "unraveling the knot," Benjamin draws the session (he draws the office, not me!) as the bearer of "gloom" (Figure 3).

Figure 2

Then, at the start of the third month, the diary entries stop recording these initial resistances and change over to the core issues of sessions and Benjamin's feelings about them. It is clear that by the third month I had moved away from the intellectual level on which we had been meeting.

I started to interpret again in the sessions, started to point out again where his theories had led him — to an

Figure 3

isolated, unhappy adolescence. He defended and, from his point of view, I attacked. I saw that I was wearing weak spots in his armor; he would become visibly angry, bristling at my remarks, and yet remain silent. I urged him to see the cost of containing his anger. But he would only cry.

Finally the diary reports: "When I went to Fred's I broke out and cried and I got really mad at him."

During that session I enraged Benjamin, but he refused to say it. He cried. I urged him to put his anger in words, but he said he couldn't. Finally, I asked him to write it down.

He wrote: "I'm getting Sick and Tired of this constant Pushing!! I've had enough!!!" (Capitalizations are his.) I thought that perhaps now, having it in writing in front of him, he would be able to overcome his fear and *be* angry with me.

So I said, "Yes, you must be very angry that I don't stop when I am upsetting you. But then why don't you tell me? Why don't you say, 'Fred, stop, don't go on'?"

As he did not answer, I pushed further. "Come on Benjamin, you hate it when I push. You think I'm being mean. You want to say, 'Shut up you bastard. Shut up you bastard.' So say it. Say it."

As Benjamin opened his mouth to say it, I could see the words that would allow his anger to break through forming in his mouth; at the same time I could see his jaw fighting him. I pushed him on, only to see the same struggle again and again. Finally he opened his mouth wide and tried to speak with all his strength. But what emerged was a throttled croak, a gasp like a choking man.

I said, "Say it," and he rasped again but more quietly, reaching for his throat, astonished, as I was, that he had lost (sic) his voice. No amount of effort on his part could produce any sound. So I told him we would have to wait until his voice returned, and we sat in silence for the remainder of the session.

I told Benjamin when the hour was up. He got up, went to the office door and opened it, then turned around and, suddenly sensing his voice had returned, said, "Goodbye, Fred."

But his rage at me, still contained, lingered on. The cartoon of the day (Figure 4) is ambiguous. Is the pain breaking through or impinging on Benjamin? But the diary entry for that day clearly concludes: "At home I was tired so I didn't do anything. I thought about how mad I was at Fred."

That was the only episode of hysterical aphasia (emo-

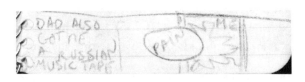

Figure 4

tionally induced loss of speech) I have ever seen. As I mulled it over in my mind, the word *hysteric* brought Freud to mind. It made me suddenly think of Benjamin as a youngster who, somehow, Freud would have been able to understand, and who, therefore, perhaps I also would understand from that point of view.

The diary, and our sessions, began to reveal other symptom "conversions."

Two weeks after the "aphasia" session the diary reveals: "At night I had a fight with Dad *so I* got a migraine [emphasis mine].

A discussion about his being overweight led Benjamin to consider a diet of "3 meals a day"[3] and after several weeks led him to consider that by being fat he was making himself look more like a girl than a boy. This session was noted in his diary and the following day's entry contained: "I've started a new exercise program to trim off fat."

Another entry contains the first reference to the transference, the first indication that Benjamin was attaching real importance to me.

Then, finally, came the revelation of Benjamin's hidden sexual life. During the third and fourth month of sessions, I had often noticed that when my gaze wandered and then returned to Benjamin he was looking at my crotch. Of course he would quickly look away, but the same thing

---

[3]Commenting on this entry several years later, Benjamin wrote: "My diet of three meals a day. How many did I eat before, five, six?"

happened over and over again. Toward the end of the fourth month I finally brought it to Benjamin's attention. He flushed hotly and said, "I do not!" but I remained firm. I told him that he was certainly not the first person to have ever "crotch gazed" and I was interested more in knowing what he was looking for than in his acknowledging that he was indeed looking.

Finally, hesitantly, Benjamin said that he wondered what I looked like naked and often fantasied that I was sitting in my chair naked. "And what do I look like?" I asked.

And he replied, "You're just naked. That's all."

But that was not all. At the very next session, now that the ice had finally been broken, Benjamin confided that he "crotch gazed" at men all the time, especially on the bus and the subway when they were in one place long enough to be stared at. He would wonder how big their penises were, wonder if he could guess by the size of the bulge in their pants.

And then he went on, "Sometimes I imagine that the man notices me staring at him, and he takes me back to his apartment. We get undressed and he has a very big penis and he fucks me." Nothing else would take place. The fantasy was always pretty much the same, one-sided and empty, and yet in some way fulfilling enough to be repeated over and over.

Benjamin's symptomatology all began to fall into a neat little Freudian row. In a most classical Freudian way he was the creation of an unresolved and continuing oedipal drama. The diary is replete with examples of this, for example his calling the parental bedroom "mom's room," referring to a gift from his parents as being from his mom, and constant references to fights with his dad and favoring his mom.

Benjamin, more than a decade later, commented on this. "One can put a Freudian cast on all this but one can also look at it from an existential point of view: I was a lonely, lost and defenseless little human being who looked into the abyss and I reacted in the only way I knew how."

But is existentialism really a different explanation, or is it only that reality often just reinforces the neurotic drama in progress? Notwithstanding his comment above, Benjamin continued, "Of course the way I knew how was in large measure dictated by an oedipal conflict: an overbearing mother and a sometimes distant, sometimes scary father. I decided to seek refuge with my mother, becoming like her, doing what she wanted me to do."

In what follows, also from the older Benjamin looking back ten years later, one can see why he chose to be close to his mother, why she appeared strong and secure:

> When my dad wasn't traveling around the country, he was at home having violent arguments with my mom. The bunk bed that my brother and I slept in was next to a wall facing the living room. Every night when I went to sleep I could hear the eleven o'clock news followed by the Johnny Carson show blaring from the television set which my parents were watching. I waited, on edge, and soon my waiting was rewarded: the snide comments would begin, then the sharp comment from my mother followed by the sharp counterattack by my father, followed by reply and counter-reply. Voices would be raised. The yelling would start. A typical night at [our] household had begun.
>
> You can imagine the fear I felt in listening to this. First there was the anticipation of the battle, hoping it would not come but knowing its inevitability. Then there was the

hope that the fight would die down quickly, or at least end in silent stalemate. As tempers rose, the hope would be that objects would not start flying, that there would be no sound of glass breaking against the wall as sometimes happened. Although occasional, my parents did exchange a few blows at times. When that happened I worried that one or the other might kill each other. . . . I still think that one reason [dad] might have taken jobs which required so much travel is that he really feared what he might do if he were home too much. . . . Then the worst fear of all— would my parents divorce? What would my life by like then? Who would I go to live with?

As I say, the fights were constant when my parents were together and the disputes erupted at any time though being most common when Mark and I were "safely" tucked away in bed (I suppose the wall between the living room and the bedroom provided some sort of illusion that the children would be unaware of the conflict). I remember fights at the dinner table. I remember fights after dinner, my brother and I coming out of our rooms to see these two red-faced human beings screaming at each other. Sometimes we would miss the main event and come out to see my father crying in my mother's arms. We would ask "What's wrong?" only to have mom softly tell us that everything would be all right and to go back to our room.

The fights were symptomatic of many problems that my parents had, the chief one being alcoholism. When dad came back from his business trips he would often bring us gifts; he would also often bring back lingering intoxication. I have one memory of dad coming back from a trip and being totally smashed. He was staggering around the room when he espied Mark and I cowering in the corner. He started to smile and say "come here" but we wouldn't come. Dad never hurt us but seeing the violent arguments he had with mom and knowing his unpredictability when drunk, we were afraid. Dad continued to call to us and then slowly walk towards us. We both backed off. He continued to call to us and walk after us and began to laugh, amused and frustrated that his own children were afraid of him.

The rage and frustration he felt was always underneath the surface, ready to explode. Thankfully, dad loved us dearly enough and had enough self-control not to physically hurt us and he usually vented his anger directly on mom. Nonetheless, the psychological damage was done.

Suffering, then, from terrible castration anxiety, Benjamin could not tolerate to have even his fingernails "cut" because it hurt. No wonder the act of trying to *be* angry with me caused hysterical aphasia. I, the new more powerful god and magician, must have been even more threatening than his father (or his mother).

It is not surprising that he had chosen to isolate himself from others and retreat to his intellectual ivory tower. He even referred to discussions with me as vigorous and strenuous, as if they were physical exertions. He had come to rely on intellectual success as the proof of his worthiness, since he felt so inadequate in every other sense. And yet, right from the first diary entry it is clear how much he had come to dislike school.[4] *Every* diary entry which begins with how tired he is falls on a school day. He is constantly counting down how many school days are left before this or another holiday. School is represented as a drudgery, a torture, and in many pictures, as a jail. Of course. The neurotic runs into a room, locks all the doors from the inside, shuts all the windows (but doesn't pull the

---

[4]Reviewing this diary entry, Benjamin wrote, "I can see I hated school."

shades down!), and sits in a corner content that he has escaped his terrors. When the sweat of his fear dries, however, he slowly comes to the realization that his "haven" is in fact a prison which *his* terror keeps him in and from which, therefore, no rescuer, no matter how brave, can save him until he himself opens the locks.

So Benjamin was trapped. As he increasingly relied on success in school to bolster his weakened sense of identity and masculinity, he became increasingly nervous about success on exams and papers. The tension, naturally, often destroyed his ability to do as well as he could. Whereas every "A," every success, held him up, anything less shot him down.

Again, a decade later, Benjamin wrote,

I hated school for the big reason that I feared failing in the one area I was a success in. Actually, my feeling then was that my academic success was a sham, that it was undeserved and that somehow failure was imminent. Bad enough that my social skills had to be tested in that setting but even worse were all the traps laid out to expose my intellectual fraud. Hence all the dreams about "tests"— beyond the sexual element, exams were devices which could expose me and scuttle my whole neurotic exercise.

No wonder then, also, his dislike of sports. A diet and/or exercise threatened to change his plump, girl-like figure into a boy's, putting him into competition where he was certain he would fail.

Certain that he was unable to be with other boys his age, Benjamin was constantly shopping, buying "things," needed or not, hoarding them, surrounding himself with them, hoping, I suppose, that in some magical way they would fill the void created by his social isolation, entertaining and distracting him from the fact of his imprisonment.[5] Most often his purchases were little proofs of his status as an intellectual, e.g., classical cassettes or books. The compulsive buying became so exaggerated, and so often discussed, that when Benjamin bought an all-Chinese dictionary the book became its own interpretation. His impression (see footnote 5) that he was buying something every day was not that far off; in the period covered by the diary, thirty-one percent of the entries mention something being purchased! There are almost as many entries mentioning eating, Benjamin's other "hoarding" technique.

But finally, the most terrible were the sexual fantasies. Here, at last and most clearly, I saw where Benjamin was (!?) going. Not yet homosexual (or any-sexual for that matter), Benjamin was already seeing the magical means by which his masculinity would be restored—through the penis and ejaculate of a man. I looked at little Benjamin and imagined him in a few years, moving from man to man, looking for the magical penis that would make him a man. I wondered if, like so many others, he would fail "to see," when he failed to become masculine, that the problem was that magic does not happen, and would instead suppose that the problem was in the penis he had selected. Then, driven by this neurotic distortion, his life would become a constant search for a bigger penis, a more powerful phallus, a more genuine man. He would forever be blind to the fact that his masculinity was inside him, could only come from inside him.

[5]Commenting on this, again several years later, Benjamin wrote, "I . . . seem to be buying something every day."

And I thought, if he becomes homosexual because that is what he is, so be it. But if he becomes homosexual in this neurotic pursuit of masculinity, his life will be destroyed. If he is really heterosexual, his search for his masculinity in this way will lead him to believe that he is gay when he is not. Since he has the intense sexual desires of an adolescent, the homosexual activity will lead him to orgasm, whether he is gay or not, further convincing him that he is homosexual, further drawing him to repeat it again and again. His heterosexuality will become repressed or he will live his life as an unhappy bisexual, tortured by his endless, unsatisfiable search for manhood. And I knew that I should prevent this if I could. But I did not know how. How could I venture into his real life and still remain neutral? How could I interfere with the unfolding of reality around Benjamin, I who am only supposed to interpret reality but not make it? And even if I could, should I, dare I?

Benjamin began to present himself in dreams, as well as in reality, as being trapped in an oedipal web from which he could not break free. He brought in an "old" dream in which he stood in a tropical hut with his family while rats ran around trying to bite him. He was overly attached to his mother and no doubt felt that his parents' marital tension was due to his feelings for her; he dreamed that she opened a window and fell out, causing his father to laugh and Benjamin to cry. Like many boys still caught up with unresolved oedipal problems at so late an age, Benjamin both needed his mother (and feared he could not live without her) and needed to get rid of her, become independent of her, in order to grow. He dreamed that he and other children (of course, at least unconsciously, he saw that his peers would be his aides) found a man enclosed in wax and melted him free.

Emotions, sexual and angry, were in turmoil within him, disrupting his perception of reality and his ability to intellectualize and sublimate. And yet he tried to convey that good could come out of his rage at his own immobility and inability to join in play with other children (see his "How the Yuletime Colors Were Chosen," in the appendix), while another part of him yearned for the freedom of motion:

The Magical Ivy

On a wall of a college a long green ivy was growing. The ivy had been there for years, watching the people go by, when, suddenly, the ivy fell off the wall and became alive. It started slithering like a snake.

The ivy explored the town. Snow was falling and there was nobody walking the streets. The ivy slithered through the streets, around corners, up walls, everywhere.

Slowly day turned to night and the ivy headed back to the college. The ivy climbed up the wall. The clock struck twelve. The magical ivy was now again just ivy.

The ivy knew, that, it became alive during Christmas day and that like everyone else, it had gotten its Christmas present, the gift of motion.

Benjamin, like the ivy, must remain just a passive observer as long as he remains attached to the wall of the college (tied to his intellectual prison). The ivy, like Benjamin, watched people (real life) go by for years until it (he) was granted a Christmas present of going for a walk (sadly, just once a year), which Benjamin correctly called becoming "alive." He wished he could know others and get about in the real world without fear of being hurt. [6]

We began to discuss his overattachment to his mother and his fear of his father's anger. We explored the difficulties that this created for him in becoming a boy and a separate person. He began to see his intellectualizations for what they were, coverups and explanations for his failures at being a boy.

And then, nine months after the beginning of therapy, Benjamin came in and told me that he wanted to tell me a dream which he had had three weeks before but had held back from revealing for the last six sessions.

> I was walking in the street with my defense attorney, who looked sort of like you. We entered a courtroom which was, in fact, my parents' bedroom. The judge, a lady, was handing out forms to be filled out and I took one. Even though she said it was a form, I knew it was a "test." I lay down on my parents' bed next to a man dressed in a military uniform who was also filling out the form and I started to fill out the test. But it kept sliding up the bed until it became lost between the bed and the wall. I went to school to look for my lost test (!), but I did not find them. I bumped into a dentist's drill (?!) which started throwing tomatoes (his association: tomatoes = red =

---

[6]"When I was [eleven or twelve] I wished I could do magic. I wished I had a genie to do my every bidding—like smite my every enemy. I wished I had a TV set that showed the future or anything I wanted to know—like when I would die. I wished I had a set to let me know what other people thought of me, and whether if I called them up they would reject me or not. I also wished I could stop time, and still move, and not grow up."

blood).[7] Two boys, who were, somehow, me, came up the front staircase, and two girls who were also me (!?) came up the *back* staircase. (Parenthetical comments and emphasis are mine.)

[7]Benjamin's terror of the dentist's drill, not surprisingly, was quite long-standing and finally became clear with this dream. In the diary, in a one-month period during which he had a few dental appointments, there are seventeen (!) references to the dentist, thinking about the dentist, or thinking about his teeth. His fear that the drill would break through his boundaries and penetrate him must have created an endless agony for him. An early cartoon depicts a much larger-than-life size drill and Benjamin with his teeth clenched (Figure 5). Even in a diary cartoon which jokingly defined a dentist as a "dent"ist (Figure 6) (how Freud would have enjoyed that) the drawing shows the "dent" in the leg; in fact, only the "legs" were drawn.

Figure 5

Figure 6

After four months of therapy the drill appeared less terrifyingly, and Benjamin, his fear lessened, opened his mouth to it (Figure 7).

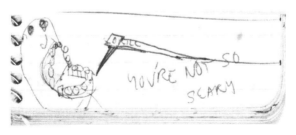

Figure 7

62

So, he lies down on the parental bed and loses his "tests." He tries to regain them (his masculinity) at school but cannot. The dream ends with blood being thrown all over, and Benjamin's first clear vision of his sexual confusion. Between us, this dream became known as "the castration dream." The relationship of the back staircase and being a girl remained, mercifully, hidden from Benjamin for the time.[8] The general implications of the dream were shocking enough. And yet, perhaps because they were so threatening, Benjamin could not truly believe in them.

The summer came and went. Benjamin began his second year in analysis. He was a little taller but still quite overweight and quite isolated.

By November his sexual development could no longer be ignored. He dreamed:

My brother and I met a gypsy. She gave us money for being kind. I gave my money back and she took out a very large-size two of spades. It didn't look like much but it turns into things. She turned it around and it was many colors. She gave me all the cards. I showed my brother the cards and I tried to stretch them, but nothing happened. Then I took the two of spades. I stretched it. Its color changed to pink and purple, and it started to give off a glow.

[8]If the reader wonders why I did not interpret this to Benjamin at this time, it is precisely because he seemed so oblivious to it. The castration elements were quite clear to him, and so we focused on them. My dear, late friend and colleague, Dr. Elisabeth Enczi, in discussing interpretations and their timing, always used to say that when Dr. Kelman, a noted analyst and teacher, was asked by his students when the right time was to make an interpretation he would reply, "The correct time to make an interpretation is two or three seconds *after* the patient makes it."

Benjamin and I both thought that stretching of the two of spades represented his getting an erection (especially because of the somewhat phallic shape of a spade — ♠); he was proud of it and glad to show it to his (younger) brother.

And yet, it was all still unreal. It all fit too neatly into the theory I had been tossing around with Benjamin for a year. It seemed right to me and I could see that he accepted it intellectually, but something was missing.

Then, in December of his second year in therapy, the reality of the oedipal triangle suddenly came alive for Benjamin. Although his efforts to grow toward independence had been very small and subtle, they must have been enough to set off tremors in the intricate webbing of his family's relationships. He told me that his mother had come to him and told him that she had had the following dream:

> She felt that Benjamin was dead and went to check on him and Mark, his younger brother. Benjamin was gone and so was the bunk bed. In its place was a crib with Mark in it.

Benjamin was very unsettled, feeling that the dream might indicate that his mother would write him off if he grew independent of her. But he realized that the forces at work both for and against him were real. How fragile and tenuous are the strands that hold together such affairs! And yet, how tenacious! It is not just our own defenses that threaten us with chaos and ruin if we try to destroy them; other people enmeshed in our neurosis for their own reasons also feel threatened and try to scare us from change too. Less than a week later, Benjamin realized this only too clearly for himself. He caught himself thinking, "I am trying to get away from mom; what happens if she tries to kill me?" He became badly frightened and imagined that she would stab him in the heart while he was asleep, or that she would poison him.[9] So he started deliberately avoiding her.[10] And then his defenses attacked in the other direction—his abandonment was making her depressed. So, she will kill him, or he will kill her.

No wonder children in these situations feel trapped. No wonder Freud imagined counteracting forces and fixation points. The "aphasia" session focused the dilemma in extremely clear relief; caught between the powerful forces pushing him toward health and against it he simply froze. The first diary entry (see p. 47) also became clearer to me. It would not be Benjamin only who would radically change; the whole house of cards would fall, and he knew it.

Benjamin turned fourteen, and the more immediate, practical difficulties of his adolescence pressed to the fore. Convinced now of the reality of his situation, Benjamin was ready to move forward. His discontent with his body and his social isolation emerged strongly. His homosexual needs pushed for realization, yet gender confusion also became apparent to him.

---

[9]Again, the terror of penetration, this time by a knife(?!)-wielding woman. And the betrayal! Murdering him while he is asleep or unaware (has she lost her power to do it while he is awake?).

[10]If she has tried to kill him psychologically, maybe she really is capable of doing it in reality.

He dreamed:

I sensed I was married. I was out but I could see my wife sitting on a couch in the living room worrying that I was not home. I came home, and we went into the bedroom.

Suddenly my wife became Mark. I said, "You're supposed to be a girl," but he replied, "No way, boy, you're the girl."

I looked in the mirror and I was dressed up as a lady. I tried to beat Mark up, and he turned back into my wife.

Suddenly, I was another guy and I stuck a pencil in my wife's eye (to blind her so she cannot see what he really is?).

He sensed that he had been hiding from his masculinity but now was looking for it. He dreamed:

I was in school (where in the "castration" dream he had been unable to find his "tests") on the last day of finals. I was unsure if I did or did not have one more test. I went to my homeroom.

An old science teacher came along and said, "I'm looking for kids who are trying to get out of their tests or are hiding out from their tests." He asked Benjamin if he was hiding out from his tests.

Benjamin replied, "No, as a matter of fact, I'm waiting for my test."

The teacher gave Benjamin a test, but just as Benjamin was about to start writing the teacher said, "Oh no, this is not your test. This is someone else's. You don't have any more tests. You can leave."

His insecurity regarding his masculinity continued, however, and he still "crotch gazed," constantly comparing himself with other boys, other men, and me.

And then, in one session, Benjamin described in detail

how he would like to have sex with another boy. Toward the end he stopped suddenly and said, "I know what you're thinking." I asked him to tell me what he thought I was thinking, and he replied, "You're thinking, 'This kid is all talk and no action.'"

His eyes suddenly examined me carefully, watching every cell on my face for a reaction, and I felt sweat break out on the back of my neck. In a moment I understood what had caused this effect; Benjamin was asking for my permission to be homosexual, for a go-ahead to act on his homosexual impulses. So I answered, "I think you are asking me for permission to be homosexual, which you know you will not get anywhere else." He nodded, and I continued, "All I can say is that no matter what you decide to do, I will still feel the same about you. I will still love you."[11]

As I drove home that night this session (which we later named the "permission" session) disturbed me deeply. On the one hand, I did not want to advise him, as such a major choice should clearly be his. And yet, what of my misgivings of just a few months earlier? If he became homosexually active now and my guess that he was heterosexual was correct, his future sexual life might be (would be?) painfully compromised. Benjamin described an even more horrible end, "Barring rape my fate . . . would have been a sort of tormented asexual existence, rich in masoch-

---

[11]Benjamin wrote that he felt I took his statement too literally. "At that point I think I was asking you for permission to act homosexually but God knows if I would have ever gotten up the courage to do anything about it. Look at the tremendous effort it took me to make a few simple phone calls to friends, and that effort was possible only after a couple of years of therapy and your necessary pushing."

istic, homosexual fantasy and longing but 'all talk and no action.'" How could I let that happen? How could I not let it happen?

Benjamin also became increasingly unhappy with his body. Although he liked his facial features,[12] his being overweight and lack of exercise had produced a shape which was embarrassing to him. He realized that, in addition, he had been neglecting his personal hygiene, not showering more than once a week and often forgetting to brush his teeth.

When I asked Benjamin why he had not ever tried dieting before, he told me that he had on many occasions. Unfortunately, after a usually successful first few days, his mother (who often helped him start the diets) would reward his self-control with a chocolate chip cookie and the diet would quickly come to an end with the "I'll just have one; can't hurt much" rationalization so often used by people who fail at dieting.[13] Benjamin's lack of exercise was related not only to his initial intellectualizations regarding the stupidity of sports but also to his confusion as to what body type he should have.

I began to realize that, if I were correct, as Benjamin developed a more solid masculine self-image his uncon-

---

[12]On a list of good and bad things about his body that we made up several months later, his facial features are essentially the only ones listed on the good side.

[13]Considering the oedipal forces at work, it should come as no surprise that Benjamin's mother was overweight, while his father was quite thin and his brother had a trim athletic build.

scious drive to achieve masculinity from the outside (from another man) would lessen, and his homosexual impulses would disappear.

I decided to start with his weight and the lack of exercise first, as I could see how I might engage Benjamin. I traded on his interest in losing weight and his compulsion with buying things. We agreed that at each session he would bring in a weight slip signed by one of his parents. For each pound he lost I paid him fifty cents; for each pound he gained he paid me fifty cents. I guess "traded" is the right word—if he had been unaware, the correct word would be "manipulation"; but, in either case (maybe I am just trying to make myself feel better by not calling it a manipulation), it was my first major foray into directly intervening with Benjamin's out-of-the-office reality. It turned out to be an excellent idea; Benjamin lost twenty-two pounds!

At the same time I knew that weight loss without exercise would not produce the results that Benjamin wanted. But I knew that it was too early to try to involve him in sports with other boys. He needed something private, where lack of skill would not be an embarrassment and success would depend on desire rather than on innate athletic ability. Benjamin's parents had just purchased a country home in a quiet corner of another state, and when Benjamin told me that they were moving many things there, including his and Mark's bicycles, we both realized that bicycling might be the activity of choice. Alone with miles of country road, little by little, Benjamin could build himself up.

As Benjamin lost weight, the bicycle trips increased in

length and difficulty. Initial runs of a few miles on level roads turned into day trips of sixty miles or more over all sorts of terrain. Years later, Benjamin's trips were for days or weeks over hundreds of miles. He found, as I had hoped, not only a way in which to develop himself unselfconsciously, but also an activity where he could move at a pace that allowed him to enjoy the world he was traversing.

Increasingly, he dreamed of being with other boys and yet always wound up alone. He dreamed:

> I was on a train with a bunch of kids I know. It looked like a subway car [going] through a dark tunnel. . . . We got off at the third stop. . . . [The other two boys] started walking off, and I was behind them. They were heading for the gate. They gained distance on me. [14]

Again, he dreamed:

> [I was in an elevator with six or seven friends.] There were three bus type handles. We went to the top floor, the 21st (2 + 1 = 3, again?). One boy went to ring a [door] bell. The door opened. Everyone went inside. I waited outside. Somehow, some of my clothes were off and I was putting them on. The kids came out and went down. I tried to dress in time but took too long. I took another elevator, but when I got to the lobby no one was there.

---

[14]Benjamin interpreted this dream as follows: "We got off on the third stop. Also, three boys were traveling, so the dream is social and sexual. The other two boys are together. I am alone." Benjamin was being left behind (outdistanced by his peers).

Three is a number usually accorded a "sexual" connotation in dreams as there are three components to the male genitalia and the female genitalia appear as an inverted triangle (a delta).

I started on a plan to help Benjamin reach out to his peers. I had him make a list of the boys whom he wanted to go out with (to the movies or a store, not sexually) and their telephone numbers. In my office he practiced dialing their numbers, rehearsing what he might say by way of invitation. Finally, after several months, I urged him to try it for real. He resisted doing it in my office, saying he would do it at home. But at home he would dial and hang up. At last he did it in my office, made a date, broke the ice.

The remaining difficulty was his homosexual "needs." While we were beginning to make progress on the other fronts, here I was stymied. If I counseled abstinence, he might see it as revoking my "permission" and betraying his trust. But, believing as I did, how could I counsel abandon, or nothing?

And then Benjamin himself provided me with the means to help. He had obtained a pornographic magazine which had photographic sequences that mirrored his homosexual fantasies. But once he had bought it, its possession hung over him like the sword of Damocles. He wanted to have it to fantasize and masturbate with, but how could he keep it at home? Every day it went into hiding, but there was always the dread that it would be discovered, the tormenting fear that when he returned from school it would be there, uncovered, along with his hidden sexuality.

And in this Gordian knot I suddenly saw something that I could do. If Benjamin left the magazine in his file at my office, then it would be available to him twice a week, but safely hidden from his family. Twice a week he could look through it, if he chose, and masturbate in the bathroom if he wanted to.[15] Perhaps this biweekly homosexual release would attenuate his needs[16] while he grew toward his own masculinity and, if I were correct, heterosexuality. If I were wrong, Benjamin would lose whatever homosexual relationships he might have had otherwise. And, I argued with myself, how many would that have been with a youngster who was just learning to make phone calls for movie dates?

I suggested this idea to Benjamin, and he jumped at it. Whatever awkwardness might arise by my knowing, in future sessions, that he was masturbating in the bathroom

[15]I had, and still have, difficulty with hard-core pornography. On the one hand, it seems obvious that many, if not all, of the models who are involved are being exploited, as well as degraded. On the other hand, research clearly demonstrates that the vast majority of those who purchase pornography use it as an aid for fantasizing and masturbation and nothing else.

[16]The experimental research, as reported in Rosen and Beck (Raymond C. Rosen and J. Gayle Beck, *Patterns of Sexual Arousal: Psychophysiological Processes and Clinical Applications*. New York: Guilford Press, 1988, pp. 200–204), on the habituation effects of repeated exposure to pornography is very inconsistent. Some studies suggest that exposure to pornography increases sexual behavior but "only those behaviors already present in the subjects' repertoires were increased" (p. 202). And Benjamin's only sexual behavior was masturbation. Another study "demonstrated that the activating effects of the erotic movies . . . declined significantly over the course of the study . . . provid[ing] evidence of habituation or satiation effects with repeated exposure, even in the face of initial increases in sexual activity" (p. 202).

Whether repeated exposure leads to satiation seems to vary with whether the stimuli presented remain constant or are varied, whether sexual release does or does not follow exposure, and other factors such as the content and intensity of the stimuli.

I do not know if Benjamin's pornographic material and masturbation reinforced his homosexual fantasies or not. I only know that as he matured he lost his need to be homosexual, and the pornography and masturbation with homosexual fantasies lost their appeal.

was overcome by his relief in being rid of the problem of having the magazine at home. So we agreed that he would bring it in at the next session, and he did. He showed me the two photographic sequences that excited him the most. The first consisted of four photographs starting with one man pressing his erection forcefully against another man's upper abdomen and proceeding higher and higher in the next two photographs until, in the last, it was inserted in the other man's mouth. The second also consisted of a sequence of photographs starting with one man lying on his back with his penis erect, another man squatting over him, and continued as the squatting man slowly lowered himself onto the other man's erection. In both sequences Benjamin saw himself as the passive recipient.

And so began a year and a half during which many sessions began or ended with Benjamin taking his magazine and fantasizing and masturbating. A year and a half of some reprieve from his homosexual drives, with the additional benefit that I was on hand to hear, and discuss, his sexual fantasies as they appeared. I came quickly to see Benjamin's need not only to receive his masculinity from another but to be dominated and controlled by another.[17] What longing for a powerful father who would keep his oedipal struggle in check! No wonder that he began to crotch gaze to "see what you've got," and started to fanta-

---

[17]Benjamin confided that, even before our sessions had begun, he had had sexual and nonsexual masochistic fantasies. In the earliest of these he saw himself naked and tied in chains to a board. He was released in order to pound rocks ("pounding your rocks" is a slang for masturbating) or forced at gunpoint to have intercourse with a woman.

In the nonsexual fantasies he saw himself as a clothed but still tied up prisoner and realized that he was a prisoner as a result of being a secret agent.

size fellating me, substituting me for the young man in his magazine.

And yet, by the end of six months, Benjamin still had not initiated any real homosexual relationships. His dieting and bicycling continued and he went out more and more often with other boys. He acknowledged that he crotch gazed much more openly now, but that he no longer found it exciting.

By the end of a year, Benjamin began to become the young man I had suspected he really was. He began to believe that he was heterosexual and now *feared* his homosexual impulses and the results of penetration. He dreamed:

> Mark and I were in our room. Mark wanted to go to a lesbian camp (?! homosexuality — one step removed [18]). I said OK.
>
> We appeared in a large place which was white and sanitary. People were on tables. The proprietress came over and told me to undress and lie on a table. Mark disappeared.
>
> I was naked on a table. Another naked guy came up to me and our neck veins somehow got intertwined, although we were lying in a 69 (mutual oral sex) position, and blood was being transferred.
>
> I was afraid this would make me a homosexual.

[18]Hatfield, Sprecher, and Traupman, in a 1978 study (as reported in Raymond C. Rosen and J. Gayle Beck, *Patterns of Sexual Arousal: Psychophysiological Processes and Clinical Applications*. New York: Guilford Press, 1988, p. 194), found that "male subjects appeared to be considerably more aroused than females to films of lesbian sexual activity." It is with this understanding that the homosexual can be very exciting to men if presented at a slight remove that heterosexual pornographers often include lesbian scenes in their magazines and movies.

Rather than involve me more in his homosexual fantasies, he began to involve me less and to see me more as a neutral observer. He dreamed:

> I was on the couch in your office masturbating. You were sitting by the door. My [pornographic] magazine was in my file but sticking up. You said, "We don't need [the] magazine." I got an erection easily.
>
> Mark came out of the bathroom. I got worried [that Mark would see] and sat up.

By the end of a year his growing belief that he was heterosexual "inside" appeared clearly in dreams:

> I was at home. I took out a pornography book with homosexual and heterosexual pictures. [It] had [a] homosexual on the cover but . . . heterosexual pictures inside.

In a year and a half his homosexual interests diminished markedly. And in the end, Benjamin never had any sexual activity with boys or men at all.

How quickly children grow and change. As Benjamin turned sixteen I no longer could recognize the little boy he had once been. Tall and strong and self-assertive, he challenged me now when he was unhappy with me, and challenged the world as well.

It started at fifteen when he no longer wanted to go to the country house every weekend. His mother insisted that he could not be left alone. They argued back and forth and finally Benjamin and his parents came in to discuss the issue. Each argument that his mother presented found a logical and ready reply from Benjamin. Finally, frustrated, she turned to me and said, "I'm just afraid that he'll have boys over, and you know how boys are, always experimenting with smoking and drinking." Alone with me later, Benjamin quickly noted how she had left out sex, but focused on her fear that he would become like other boys, if only by imitation. I think his father must have sensed this too and come to his son's aid by becoming our ally in winning this privilege for Benjamin. Benjamin, of course, rose to the challenge. Others were not invited to parties while his parents were gone, the apartment did not burn down, he did not lock himself out; he became self-sufficient, street-wise, independent.

By sixteen, challenging me and his parents was not enough. Sensing (as countless other adolescents have!) that his school was censoring its newspaper, he challenged its sponsors. When they turned a deaf ear, he organized a group of ten other students and started publishing his own independent newspaper. The lead story in the first issue was a genuine piece of investigative reporting, complete with allegations of improprieties, interviews with disaffected students, and a rebuttal. He managed to bring out this paper more regularly than the school did theirs and expanded its investigative scope to other schools.

He helped organize a political discussion group and began to get actively involved in the well-being of the poor and the defenseless. His alternate newspaper devoted the entire editorial page of one issue to a reasoned plea for students to boycott a company after a scandal broke regarding the corporation's dealings with third world countries.

He began to make his first efforts toward girls, although he knew he would be awkward compared to other boys his age. He began to consider what colleges he might apply to, and in sessions we began to discuss the end of therapy. Benjamin and I both felt that we had accomplished the goals that we had set for him. He was honest with others, sensitive, and self-confident. His homosexual impulses continued to decrease in frequency and intensity. I knew he still had far to go, but it was a distance I felt confident he could walk without me. We planned a last session and had paté and champagne with it to celebrate.

I kept in contact with Benjamin during his senior year in high school, but it was not necessary to meet for any sessions. Usually he would call and let me know what was new in his life, his latest adventure or accomplishment. He continued to develop in all the areas we had worked on, and every phone call from him was a pleasure. I still worried (but to myself) about how he would fare among the more sexually and socially adept at college.

His freshman year went well. There were the usual academic and social ups and downs, but Benjamin made a few friends. Toward the end of the year there was a failed attempt to develop a relationship with a girl. The effect of this attempt carried over into the beginning of his sophomore year, and was a factor, from my point of view, in his decision to take part in a second semester transfer program to another college. He was socially well accepted there but his first attempt to date failed. Yet his letter to me about it revealed his newfound attitude:

I asked her with very little nervousness though. I went in with the frame of mind of "I like her, I want to get to know her better, let me see if she wants to get together and do something" and it greatly alleviated my fear. Unfortunately, she . . . promised to call back with a response but never called back. I was upset for a while but "C'est la vie." Rome wasn't built in a day.

By the spring, however, Benjamin had met another girl and started dating seriously. As the end of the school year approached, and they grew toward being lovers, Benjamin's anxiety rose dramatically. He called. It seemed clear that, as much as he wanted to have a sexual relationship, he was still terrified of the physical contact. We discussed his fear in terms of his castration anxiety[19] and dread of penetration, as well as in terms of much more normal worries (will I satisfy her sexually?). He had a clear understanding of this now and needed no interpretation from me. We talked about ways in which he could begin to learn what might please her sexually. In the end, he realized that he would just have to relax and face his fear.

They had, at her suggestion, been sleeping together for several nights with no demand or expectation that he perform sexually. I thought that was an excellent idea and assured Benjamin that nature would take her course.

Benjamin called again a week later. After a few more days of easing himself into it, he and his girlfriend had finally had intercourse four times. As he put it, "I guess I'm technically not a virgin anymore." It was so typical of him still to put such a black-and-white category in such hesitant terms. I teased him a little about this, and he laughed.

[19]For instance, "I will put my penis in, but nothing will come out."

Benjamin L.

He told me that I had been right in assuring him that he would experience ecstasy in letting go and losing control. His girlfriend told him that he was quite good, and he was exhilarated. How lucky he was that that was his first experience — gentle, exciting, wonderful, and slow.

As if having intercourse had finally laid the castration neurosis aside along with its attendant oedipal problems, Benjamin reported that on their final night together (i.e., after the successful love-makings) he had a sexual dream involving his mother (and, tangentially, his brother); even he was impressed that now the dream came uncensored, with no more of the carefully disguised details of earlier oedipal dreams he had had. He dreamed:

> I was lying in bed with my mother. She was sitting cross-legged staring at me, her lower torso covered by a sheet. I was lying up on my stomach in front of her, my upper body supported by my two arms which were holding me up, and my lower body covered by a sheet. We were talking about and preparing to have sex.
>
> To be a bit more descriptive, the bed was actually a mattress tucked away in a corner of the room. On either wall against which the bed was touching, there was a big glass window (so the world can see in?). At the foot of the bed was a screen door (even the door can be seen through!). Outside, there was a lawn and a number of trees. It was a sunny day.
>
> As my mother and I were talking, I looked out the window and I saw my brother walking towards the house, carrying a six-pack of Coca-Cola. When he reached the door, I reached up, turned the doorknob and let him in, hoping that if I did that he would not be mad. When he saw us, he had no visible reaction, but turned around and ran. My mother and I hypothesized that he might be mad

and when he joined in to play football with a bunch of guys outside, we concluded that we were right since we thought that Mark was playing ball to get his aggression out.

Suddenly the dream turned sour. My mother was out of bed. She was naked and was walking away from me. I was sitting down and crying and was feeling terribly remorseful about what I had done. I wondered how I could ever patch things up with Mark. My mother threw something that looked like a phonebook in my lap and told me to stop crying. She said there were plenty of bad things going on in the world in an attempt to justify my action. (Parenthetical remarks are mine.)

In spite of the fact that so much more would yet have to happen to and for Benjamin, this lovely sexual and symbolic duo of events had, for all intents and purposes, brought to an end a most Freudian case.

Several more years passed. Benjamin graduated from college. He and his girlfriend were both working, and living together. I saw them together for lunch or dinner. I visited their first apartment, reminded pleasantly by it of my own earliest one.

Within months of each other I received invitations to their engagement party and to their wedding.

As I sat at Benjamin's wedding, the warmest and most wonderful feelings came over me. I was proud of him and how he had grown and so thankful that he had come to believe in his ability to love and be loved. I stood delight-edly with the other guests to toast to his happiness.

Is this, then, what psychoanalysis is all about? Yes. Yes! Congratulations, Benjamin. Here's to your life. To life! L'chaim.

HOW THE YULETIME COLORS WERE CHOSEN

A long, long, long time ago, an old man was chosen to choose the colors of Christmas, by a high power called the director of Holidays.

At first the Old man chose brown because a tree is somewhat brown and everyone uses a christmas tree.

Then he decided blue would be a good color because a tree needs water.

Then he decided to use white because at Christmas eve everyone looks out to the sky and the stars are white.

Then he saw the children running out to play with thier toys.

He tried to do the same but he found he was too old.

He turned Green with Envy, and all he could see was red.

So that's how the yuletime colors came to be green and red.

3

ALEX B.

On the Importance of
Moving Slowly

PREFACE

In April 1982, my dear friend and colleague, Dr. Elisabeth Enczi, died after a brief illness. For me she was, and will always remain, a marvelous embodiment of the best that psychoanalysts and psychoanalysis can be. In the year following her death, an award was established in her memory to be given out each year for the best paper submitted about psychoanalysis.

It was while looking on the bookcase in my office that the author of the following chapter, a thirteen-year-old patient at the time, spied the award announcement for 1984 and asked me what it was about.

"Do you have to be a psychoanalyst to submit a paper?" he asked.

"No," I replied. "It's just for the best paper about psycho-analysis."

"Then I'd like to write one," he said.

Because Alex was not a very proficient typist, I suggested that he dictate while I typed. I had no idea, then, what he would choose to write about. He worked in this way, on and off, for two years, only to begin again and finally finish when he was eighteen and about to leave for college. The footnotes, unless otherwise noted, were added by me with Alex's permission, as was the final small piece.

In the interim, the other chapters in this book were written, and I began to nourish the hope that Alex would allow me to use his paper as the center chapter. For me, the change of voice here is very important. It grounds this book. It speaks with the clarity and honesty of the young and without any of the pretensions of the old. Without it, readers might come away from what they are reading here and say, "That Berenstein is good with fairy tales." Alex's chapter makes it clear that the others are true stories built from the same basic materials as his.

"What is REAL?" asked the Rabbit one day, when they were lying side by side near the nursery fender, before Nana came to tidy the room. "Does it mean having things that buzz inside you and a stick-out handle?"

"Real isn't how you are made," said the Skin Horse. "It's a thing that happens to you. When a child loves you for a long, long time, not just to play with, but REALLY loves you, then you become Real."

"Does it hurt?" asked the Rabbit.

"Sometimes," said the Skin Horse, for he was always truthful. "When you are Real you don't mind being hurt."

"Does it happen all at once, like being wound up," he asked, "or bit by bit?"

"It doesn't happen all at once," said the Skin Horse. "You become. It takes a long time. That's why it doesn't often happen to people who break easily, or have sharp edges, or who have to be carefully kept. Generally, by the time you are Real, most of your hair has been loved off, and your eyes drop out and you get loose in the joints and very shabby. But these things don't matter at all, because once you are Real you can't be ugly, except to people who don't understand."

"I suppose you are Real?" said the Rabbit. And then he wished he had not said it, for he thought the Skin Horse might be sensitive. But the Skin Horse only smiled.

"The Boy's Uncle made me Real," he said. "That was a great many years ago; but once you are Real you can't become unreal again. It lasts for always."[1]

From The Velveteen Rabbit *by Marjorie Williams*[2]

I'd spent time with psychiatrists before, when I was really little, and I hated it—I didn't hate them personally but I just didn't like the way they did things and I wanted to write about that.

The first time I saw a psychiatrist I was probably four. I was too young to remember why. It was most likely because of my parents' divorce that I needed to see someone. I suppose something must have happened that made them decide to send me there but I don't remember specifically what it was. I just remember getting up and going. I

[1] Alex—"In psychoanalysis the friendship becomes real."

[2] Williams, Margery (Hague Michael, Illus.). *The Velveteen Rabbit: Or How Toys Become Real.* New York: Holt, Rinehart and Winston, 1983, pp. 4–5.

After Rick read me this story and saw that I liked it, he bought me a copy of the book. I kept it at my dad's house, but I didn't let him see it; I tucked it away.

Then my dad was doing a version for TV and later said that he wanted to read me the story. Of course I pretended that I had never heard of it before. So he brought me a copy but didn't read it to me. We didn't talk about it at all. It was just because he was doing the show.—Alex

was between five and seven the first time I saw a lady alone and then again once or twice with my parents present.

Then in third grade I saw a man and that was the first time I was really conscious of what I didn't like about it.

It was just so clinical; it was so cold. I sat across from him, and it was a big room; he had one chair over here, one chair over there and you sat across from him. He'd just come out with questions as if he was reading them off, and that's about it. He'd ask a question and I'd usually come up with an answer. I can't remember whole sessions, I just remember the feeling of not wanting to speak to somebody who I didn't know, who I wasn't friends with. It was just something that I had to do once a week.

A lot of times I wouldn't tell him the truth. I mean I didn't lie all of the time, it's just that some things I didn't feel like talking to a stranger about. I just would come up with something else or leave something out. I can't remember specifics, I just remember not always wanting to get into things with him, because I didn't feel like talking to somebody I didn't know. I don't think anybody does.

I guess he didn't get anywhere. I guess we didn't get anywhere at least I don't think that we did. I saw him during the school year. The summer came up with camp and after that I didn't see him again.

In fourth grade I didn't see anyone. I came to Rick in sixth grade. I was self-referred. [3]

So, I had been to psychologists before and always had left with the same question on my mind. . . . "Why do I bother?" It seemed that the more that I would go to the

[3] In the initial session (when Alex's parents were still there), I asked why he was there and his mother said, "Alex said he wanted to talk to somebody because he's been having dreams that are bothering him."

doctor's office the more I would ask myself just what I had accomplished. I thought that Rick would be just the same as the others. I went into the session willingly but without much interest. I was pretty sure that he would be just like the others. There would be no harm in wasting one hour of my time every week if it would appease my parents. Once in his office I became very aloof. I sort of shut myself off from what Rick and my mother were saying.

I remember, I could never look anybody in the eye and when we were first alone he changed that right away. This was a bad habit that I had had for many years. I never used to look people in the eye—it made me so nervous. I found it very distressing to have someone look right into my eyes. It gave me the feeling that I was being seen through. If you don't let people look directly into your eyes they can't see through you. The only people I ever looked in the eyes were my friends and my parents; I didn't do it with teachers or strangers. And so when I came to Rick's office I remember looking up at the track lights, looking at each one—squinting my eyes to see the light rays. I was just playing around. Finally Rick got my attention and asked me why I always looked at the ceiling or the walls when he talked to me.[4]

It was something big, something that never really had occurred to me but as soon as he said it I knew, and I thought, "Wow, that's strange."

---

[4]I said, "I would appreciate it if you looked at me and not look at . . . I'm not over there where the bookcase is. I'm here in front of your face."

And Alex said, "I have a little trouble with it."

And I just said, "Yes, I know. I can see that. But all the more reason for trying to look at me."

I decided that it would not hurt to look directly at him just this once. At first it bothered me but soon I began to feel very comfortable. I suppose that to some people this may sound extremely insignificant but it made me believe that there was something different about Rick. By making me look directly at him he forced me to confront him and deal with him. I could not avoid him now because he could see right into me. This was the beginning of our friendship.

I knew that there was something different about Rick and with a little more enthusiasm I was ready for another session. I could tell he was unlike the others; it might have been little things, but I never even thought of that before. He even talked differently; it wasn't like, well, it was just different from the last guy. Everything seemed a little slower; he didn't just jump into it like the last guy. It wasn't like something he could just punch into a computer and change but that's the way the other guy had made it seem. I felt so far away from the other guy. It may have just been the way we sat, but the other guy seemed to be talking about something different than I was. But Rick didn't do it like that. It wasn't just quick.

I remember, it was after a month or so, he still moved slowly and if he didn't he repeatedly apologized. And he also bothered me if I apologized.[5] It was true, though; I

---

[5] I think a youngster who's always apologizing, who's always excusing himself, feels like there's something wrong with him. I definitely felt the apologizing reflected Alex's feeling poorly about himself and I didn't want to be a participant in that. Besides, some of the time you honestly cannot be apologetic, in which case it's false. So I try to minimize that by saying that politeness has its place but it can be exaggerated. Certainly in this office its place is a very minor place and definitely comes second to honesty.

did apologize a lot. I apologized for everything. I would apologize for the smallest things, because they didn't seem small. I thought everything was a big thing. If I dropped a cake at my mom's house, I would have to clean it up; she wouldn't scream at me, but still . . . it was something that was pounded into my head—I don't know where from. Maybe that could have been from when my mom got divorced? The feeling that it was my fault and I always had to apologize. I still do it. [6]

I understood what Rick was saying but I still had the habit and apologized for small things, but less so with him. I guess it becomes that way with all people who are your friends; you don't have to apologize for everything, it's understood. So that may have been something that just happened with time, as we became friends.

The first time I ever saw a shrink my parents were there and all we really talked about was this dream I had, I guess I should call it a nightmare.

In the dream I was eating dinner with my mom and dad in the mountains and there was a lot of snow there and there was a little blue bird and he was sitting around outside walking in the snow and we were putting our coats up on a rack and we sat down. My father's coat was a big fur coat he rarely wears. But my mom's coat fell. And she got up to put it back. She got up for some reason; I know she didn't just get up for nothing. Just then there was a big roar outside and a huge round boulder came in right through

---

[6]When Alex wrote that he still apologized a lot, he was only thirteen or fourteen. This difficulty diminished as he grew older.

the door and my mom *wouldn't* move and it ran right over her. And she went out the door with it. That's it.

I don't remember what the lady said about it. I don't remember if she even knew or had a clue about what it meant. At the time he [Rick] said that it had something to do with my parents getting divorced. That maybe I would lose my mom.

In another dream, again definitely a nightmare, I lost my dad. We were walking together up a mountain path. I saw a hooded figure behind us with an axe. And he threw it at my dad's back. My dad fell down onto the side of the cliff. I tried to pull him back up but I didn't have the strength. I let go. [7]

[7]The original versions of Alex's dreams as I have them in my notes:

"I was in Snowbird, Utah with my mom and dad and a boulder came down and ran over my mom."

Alex and his father were walking on a dirt path with a cliff on the side. A man wearing a monk's brown robe with a hood approached his father from behind. The place where his face was was all black. Alex could see no hands. The man threw an axe (as drawn by Alex it was a double-edged axe) at Alex's father. The axe stuck in his back in the middle and he fell over the cliff. Alex jumped at his father, trying to catch him, but grabbed onto the side of the cliff instead. He tried to let go of the cliff but he couldn't.

As Alex now retold the dream involving his mother's being carried off, I was struck by the fact that he remembered that they had first all sat down and that then his mother had gotten up to get her coat or something. In the first telling of this dream two years before (see original earlier in this note) this detail had been left out. As soon as Alex mentioned it, I thought, "I wonder if he will now realize that both dreams involve not only his fear of losing his parents, but also his rage at them for divorcing each other and splitting up his world. I wonder if he will suddenly see that in both dreams he is the murderer." Just as this thought finished crossing my mind I heard Alex draw in his breath sharply, and I knew, before I turned around, why he had stopped speaking.

Just as I got to this point in the retelling of my dreams, I suddenly became extremely upset. I drew in a sharp breath. Rick, who was typing as I dictated, turned around.

"Alex," he said, "What's the matter? Why are you crying?"

I replied, "I killed him. I tried to pull him back up on the road, but when I couldn't, I let go."

I started to cry more and Rick hugged me and said, "I know, Alex, I know." He held me for a while until I stopped crying and then he said, "Enough of this for now."

I think that I was wrong now, but I used to think that maybe we were moving too slowly.[8] My dad would often inquire what we had discussed during the last session as I would always go to his house after the sessions. He would also often be slightly upset that I would come home later

---

[8]Some thoughts on going too slowly: When there is going to be pain, there is always reluctance on my part to move my patient to it, and I slow down from my twenty miles an hour to ten miles an hour, and distract myself and make diversions. For it hurts me as much, if not more, because I have to go through it twice. So, generally it only goes too slowly here after a certain period of time if I'm reluctant to go forward, in which case I slap myself on the wrist and push myself on.

But I always liked the pace that Alex and I had. It was a good pace because it always went forward, but not so fast forward that when I screwed up I couldn't apologize my way out of it. I wasn't steamrolling ahead so there wasn't major damage being done along the way. If you're moving at the right tempo, then forays, mistaken forays, or forays into dead ends are very minor ones and don't do any harm.

than the session was scheduled to end. I felt that my dad thought that we should just be solving problems, something that you could just do. I felt that he was pushing us to just "straighten this kid out and forget it," that's it. And that wasn't happening here. And now I realize that it wasn't so close to happening then, but at first I guess I thought that it should. That's the way it was with the last psychiatrist, as if he was just going to diagnose a problem, find a cure, and get me out. Even with the other psychiatrist my dad would say, "What did you do today?" Or he would always ask, "What did you get done today?" As if each day was supposed to accomplish something on the road to my recovery, and it wasn't happening. And I would say, "Oh, the usual" or, "Nothing." And after my sessions with Rick when my dad would ask I would say, "We just talked." He would ask about what and I would avoid the question.

At this time, however, Rick had started reading some fairy tales to me. I would have been embarrassed if anyone had known, but I wasn't because nobody did; I was afraid that there was something wrong with it, as if Rick shouldn't be doing that because I was twelve years old. I enjoyed hearing the fairy tales, but I worried when I got to thinking about it, or what my dad would say if he heard about it. I think he would have disapproved because twelve was too old for fairy tales. But maybe it was right since I had missed them when I should have gotten them. I mean nobody ever read me fairy tales when I was young, at least not that I can remember.[9] It was like stopping the

[9]How reading the fairy tales began.

He looked at a book on the wall, and I said, "Are you looking for anything special?"

clock and going back to when I should have had them read to me; but then it was always back to reality—the same fucking world. [10]

I guess that sounds bitter, but then I was a very bitter child. I guess the reason was because afterwards I would always go to my father's house and at that time that was very difficult. Once a month, at least, I would usually be in some sort of a fight with him, and I would end up storming out of his house and going over to my mother's. So, I wouldn't want to leave Rick's because I knew I would be going straight to dinner at my dad's and then there would either be silence or we would be talking about whatever it was we were fighting about. And I didn't look

---

And he said, "No."
I asked, "Do you like fairy tales?"
And he replied, "I don't know."
And I said, "Do you have a favorite fairy tale?"
And he said, "No."
"Did you ever read fairy tales?"
"Not really."
"Well then, I'll read you some."

[10]The session after Alex dictated the material about the fairy tales was our last one before a summer break. I asked Alex why, if he had thought my reading fairy tales was wrong, he had not said anything to me. His reply was his most enigmatic smile, and so I suggested that perhaps it was another example of his inability to question grown-ups for fear that he would anger them. Alex gave this interpretation an unconvincing "maybe" and when I said I wasn't convinced he buried his head under the cushions on the couch. I laughed and said that he was not going to get away without answering me, especially as this was our last session for a while.

Finally, after more prodding with "Why didn't you tell me?," Alex looked up from the cushions and said, "Because I was afraid you would stop."

forward to that. I didn't want to fight with him, and I didn't want to go home. [11]

After the first year of therapy, Rick said that I had been very honest and personal about myself and that he wanted to let me know more about himself. So, he told me the story of the snow leopard which was about a patient of his and their relationship. After this I told him a secret of my own.

It may sound silly but it was about an imaginary secret room that I had in the apartment in which my parents lived when they were married. The entrance to the room was through a hatch in the middle of my bedroom floor. You had to climb down a ladder. Rick and I spent a lot of time talking about the room, and we decided that there were three walls in the room. To your right, there was a large central panel; there were many TV screens on it and buttons. To the right of that was a bunk bed. The whole room was brown, dark panelled wood. There was another wall, but I don't know what was on it because I never looked at it. The one with the switches had controls and rockets and bombs. I would use the control panel to shoot rockets off, and that was basically how I was controlling my anger.

---

[11]On several occasions when their battles were very painful, Alex would plead to stay. But we both knew he could not. I would say, "I understand, but you have to go or your father will be even more angry." Of course, my personal bent would be to say, "So call him up and tell him you're not coming, you're staying here for dinner and you'll sleep here." When Alex was older and he actually did stay at the office a couple of times, it caused quite a ruckus.

But one time, after I had been dreaming about this room for about six months, I went up the ladder, and there was a space between the roof of the dream room and the floor of my bedroom. In the space there were millions of roaches. It was apparent that there were enough cockroaches to fill the room up. I was scared to go through but if I didn't I would have been trapped in the room forever.[12] So as quickly as I could I ran up the ladder and broke outside. I knocked all the roaches off of me and killed them except for a few that escaped. While doing that I saw myself in the dream from above. So I never went down there, never again. I never went down again. I was five years old.[13]

----

[12]At this point Alex looked up and asked me, "What would have happened if I had been too afraid?" and I suggested that when he would have woken up he would still have been, psychologically, in the secret room, i.e., it would have been "real" and he would have been delusional.

Either he had to stay there in the place where the anger was and it was clearly visible to him, or he had to get away from it. He had either to be on one side or the other side and access would always be impossible afterwards, in either direction.

[13]When Alex stopped I asked, "What do you think of the room now?" and when he answered that he didn't know I asked, "What were you controlling? What were the rockets going off?"

"My anger," he answered.

"What was on the wall you never looked at?"

"My anger."

It is interesting to note, again, that in the first revelation of the secret room (one year before) Alex never mentioned his dramatic escape from the roaches, *nor* the fact that that was his *final* visit to the secret room. I was allowed to see the mechanism with which he controlled his anger but not the circumstances which so frightened him psychologically that he lost access to it.

I mean by this that in the original telling of the dream the mechanism, the fact that he could clearly see that you can control your anger,

It has been a long time since I have written anything for this paper. My relationship with Rick has changed; he is no longer my shrink who is "so cool" or "the best." He is my best friend. If anyone asked me, this would definitely be said.

I guess it started from the very first session with eye contact and I realized that nobody else had ever noticed this and no one had ever bothered to say anything about it. So I thought that was pretty cool. And then little things like the way things were conducted in the office. We both sat on the couch or we sat wherever we wanted, or we'd eat there. Time wasn't fixed, it was relaxed. Sometimes we'd play a game, and other times we'd play chess or go out and get something to eat. It was not like I was just coming to some kind of a talk. It was like going over to a friend's house to hang out and talk about things.

I can't say what path my life would have taken up till now had I not seen Rick. Certainly things would have been different because there were times when I had very big problems with my father and mother at the same time, or either one. And I don't have a very easy time talking to either one of them so I really would have had nobody to talk to worth the dime for the phone call because anyone

---

that there was a place in which he could go internally which had levers and buttons which controlled whether the rockets went off or not, was shown, but it was only in the retelling of the dream that this dramatic final version of the dream was revealed and it became clear to me that the control room was no longer accessible to him, the anger was no longer directly visible and controllable and had become repressed and was evidencing itself in other ways.

else would have been a peer and though they would have been good to talk to, I wouldn't have gotten the good advice and understanding that I got from Rick. If I was uncomfortable with something, Rick would pursue it for a little while, then give up and then bring it up later, and then sometimes talk about something that was bothering him. And that's sort of the point I guess, that I really came to trust him as a friend. Sometimes I'd walk in the office and he'd start complaining about some problem, and that was more than I would hear from some psychiatrist. We often would spend half of the session or more talking about something that happened to him during the week. I liked it when we talked of each other's problems instead of only mine, because then we were talking as equals. It is a nice feeling when a "grown-up" asks your opinion on something or confides in you. It is especially nice when you know that your opinion is being taken seriously. It was a real relationship.

I thought that it was important (to write this chapter) so that people would know how I thought it should be done, because I felt that I'd gone to other psychiatrists and it was done wrong. I did get something done with Rick, and it was because we moved slowly and because we became friends, instead of immediately jumping into a hot or cold tub and trying to solve a problem. And yet I did work out the problems I had, problems with myself and with my family, and learned to understand what they were about.

To understand this better I think I should explain what the qualities of a best friend are to me. A best friend must always be listening, always caring and loving, always there, tolerant, never lying, and always accepting. Rick is all of these to me. I have never met a person other than Rick with all of these qualities. They are very hard to fulfill.

For instance . . . caring. One winter vacation I was going skiing in St. Anton, Austria. While I was away skiing, he heard on the radio that there were avalanche problems in another area with a similar name but which is, in fact, far, far away from where I was. After hearing this he got worried and called my mother to see if she had spoken to me and if I was OK. This shows his worry, and one worries for someone he or she cares about.

Then, listening. . . . One night as he was driving me home, we passed an art gallery and I saw a painting or poster of two black panthers in high grass. I mentioned that I liked it a lot and that's all. Then we drove off and there was nothing more said of the poster. A few months later for my birthday I received that as my present. It was so great that he remembered that casual mention of the poster.

I think it's obvious that he is always listening, seeing that he is a psychoanalyst, but when he has a theory on something there is always room for mine.

He's very tolerant, too. This chapter's an example. I did give him my word that I would finish it last summer and here I am now (a year later).

The "always there" part, that's really important because a best friend is somebody you can always count on to do something if there's ever something they can do to help you.

Accepting . . . this to me is the most important of all. It is also the hardest of all. I'm sure there are things that, well, at least with me there are things that I wouldn't tell certain people about myself because they wouldn't be able to accept them. They'd say, "All right," but they would feel differently about me. Gradually I learned that it was different with Rick, because some things I wouldn't want to say and I'd say them and he didn't get pissed off. Little by little as I went along I tested him out. I know that I could do anything and I could tell Rick, and no matter what it was, or how horrible it was, he would still feel the same way about me as he does.

I'm going away to college soon and I'll miss him a lot. I know that I'll still see him a lot; I'll still speak to him a lot. It's going to be just the way as with the other people who are my good friends. There are those who I know I'll lose touch with after we graduate. And there are some people who will always come first. And Rick is one of those people.

This chapter is Alex's, but he has unselfishly allowed me to add the final words.

Alex at eighteen.

We are sitting on the couch and I notice an insect crawling across the carpet. It is black and bigger than a large ant, and I say, "There's a bug on the carpet."

Alex gets up, takes out his wallet and holds it so the insect can walk onto it. Then he carefully walks over to the patio door, opens it, and deposits the bug outside.

How can I express how I will miss this gentle, kind soul?

The heart breaks.

4

JEFFREY N.

Shamed to Silence

PREFACE

*At the time that I began seeing Jeffrey N., the issues sur-
rounding child sexual abuse were just beginning to be seriously
discussed and brought to public attention. Since that time many
of these issues, especially ones involving the validity of "recovered" memories, have been whipped into a frenzy by the media,
creating an atmosphere not totally unlike what apparently existed during the Salem witch trials. Unhappily, as at the time of
those trials, the focus has been on the trials, rather than the
children. Jeffrey and I kept the focus on him, where I believe it
should always be. I cannot see how anything else I might have
done could have helped Jeffrey in any way. I hope the reader
will agree.*

*This book is not the place to discuss the issues of recovered
memories. Let me only mention that even memories of traumatic*

events can be quite distorted and inaccurate. There is growing evidence that people can easily come to believe total fabrications when these are suggested to them by people they trust. This has been shown several times in the research studies done by Dr. Elizabeth Loftus and her colleagues[1] and reported on in The New York Times *("Miscoding Is Seen as the Root of False Memories," May 31, 1994). "Facilitated communication," where previously uncommunicative autistic children and adults are suddenly able to type on a computer with the help of a "facilitator," has fared no better under scientific scrutiny. The entire June 1994 issue of the* Journal of Child Abuse and Neglect *deals only with this one issue. To quote researcher Steve Heckler, "None of our evaluation techniques . . . produced any independent communication. We could . . . easily steer a response and* **did so on every occasion**"[2] *(emphasis mine).*

The real issue in therapy, however, is not whether memories are true or false. Freud, often accused of not believing his patients when they told of abuse, knew this as well. What he did believe was that the only important thing was whether or not his patients believed in their memories and the effects that this belief had on their lives. Freud's great discovery of the power of the

[1]Loftus, E. F. "The Repressed Memory Controversy." *American Psychologist*, 1994, 49, pp. 443–445.

Loftus, E. F. "Near-natal Memories, Past-life Memories, and Other Memory Myths." *American Journal of Clinical Hypnosis*, 1994 (Jan), 36 (3), pp. 176–179.

Loftus, E. F. "The Reality of Repressed Memories." *American Psychologist*, 1993, 48, pp. 518–537.

Loftus, E. F. "When a Lie Becomes Memory's Truth: Memory Distortion After Exposure to Misinformation." *Current Directions in Psychological Science*, 1992 (Aug), 1 (4), pp. 121–123.

Loftus, E. F., and Hoffman, H. G. "Misinformation and Memory: The Creation of New Memories." *Journal of Experimental Psychology: General*, 1993, 118, pp. 100–104.

[2]Heckler, S. "Letter to the Editor." *Journal of Child Abuse and Neglect*, 1994, 18 (6), p. 540.

unconscious mind showed him that men's lives are driven not by rational thought, the common view at the time, but by inner beliefs, no matter how irrational.

Knowing this, even when we can never know if the apparent memories are accurate, there is little chance we will become "deaf to the voices of adults who were abused as children."[3] As clinicians, we will always be open to hear our patients' stories, because they reveal what our patients believe about themselves, and these beliefs are the keys to understanding their lives and our guides in trying to help them.

Readers of this chapter might wonder why I didn't encourage Jeffrey to take legal action. In great part this was because Jeffrey, like many sexually abused boys, did not want his family to know what had happened to him and would have refused to testify at a trial. Although his neurotic difficulties were eventually resolved during therapy, I came to believe that Jeffrey would need this very privacy as part of his process of healing fully. And that process can take a long time, often years past the end of therapy. Indeed, it was not until eight years after Jeffrey and I finished our work together that he finally felt able to share his story with someone else. He gave a draft copy of this book to his girlfriend, and they read and discussed the first chapter. Several days later he handed the book to her, opened to his chapter, and asked her to read that chapter next. When she asked why he wanted her to read that particular chapter, he replied, "because then you'll know a great deal more about me."

This chapter was a joint effort. The sections in italic were written by me, but Jeffrey did not see them until the end. Jeffrey wrote the rest.

[3]Hopenwasser, K. "When It All Comes Back." *The New York Times*, June 8, 1994, p. A25.

Jeffrey N.

Once upon a time there was a little boy of six or seven. He lived in a happy world full of fun and adventure. He was very brave and independent. And then one day a mean and terrible sorcerer invited him to his castle to play with his trains. And when the little boy left, when it was all over, his world was no longer full of fun and adventure, and he was no longer so brave. Instead, the world was dark and lonely, and he felt very bad about himself. I know. I was the little boy.

Jeffrey N.

Six years later I was twelve. My dad always went out with some friends on Thursday nights for a "boys night out." He told my sister that he would be home at eleven. But it was two in the morning when my mother woke me to ask if I knew where my dad was. He didn't come home until five thirty.

Those three and a half hours were the longest and most hurtful time I have ever spent.

After he came home I still couldn't sleep. The terror was still inside of me; the terror that he was missing and would be missing forever; the terror that I would never know what had happened to him.

Two weeks later I was walking my dog in Central Park, and one man shot another man through the face. I saw him lying on the ground with blood rushing out of his cheek.

My terror that the members of my family might leave and never come back got worse. Each time someone left I felt that I would never see them again. I took many precautions when they were leaving; I always wanted to know where they were going and precisely when they were coming back. But it didn't help; it only made me worry more often. My family thought it was a drag; they didn't understand what I was going through.

Finally, after a month, my mother talked to a pediatrician who suggested that I see a psychoanalyst. And so I went to meet Rick.

I arrived at Rick's office frightened but relieved. I didn't know what would happen; I expected that it would be like a doctor's office, all white and uncomfortable. But it was the exact opposite. It looked like he lived there; it was a very comfortable room with many windows and very spacious. After asking me some basic questions, Rick asked me about the trouble I was having when people left the house. I suddenly burst into tears, but I couldn't tell Rick why. I only remember asking him not to tell my mother that I had been crying. Although I didn't feel totally comfortable with him, I agreed to see him again.

I did go again, even though I thought it was pointless. I asked Rick if there was something that he could give me to stop me from worrying. He laughed and replied, "I wish there were."

I told Rick that my parents fought almost every day and I thought that that was the problem. Also, my mom and my older brother fought a lot. Once they fought because my mom wouldn't let my brother make a phone call. They were at each others' throats and my mother threatened to call the police. I felt like fainting. I begged her not to call. If the police took him to a juvenile place I didn't think I could handle it. The last thing I needed was someone missing from my family.

Another time my mother and father got into a fight about my brother. My mother threatened to leave and went to pack her bag. My father offered to get my brother his own apartment instead, but my mother was determined to leave. I was taking a nap; my brother woke me and said, "Mom's leaving," knowing that I would try to stop her. Again I begged her to stay. She did.

I told Rick, "It's too much pressure on me. I feel that I'm holding the whole family together."

As Jeffrey lives on the Upper West Side and is only twelve, I decided to offer him a ride on my way home. He thanked me but wanted to call home to make sure that it was all right. On the way, as we passed through a tunnel in the 79th Street park transverse, Jeffrey confided that sometimes he gets a very strong impulse to destroy something — "'Like if you gave me a very expensive watch, I would start to squeeze it just to see when it would break, but then I would be afraid that I would really break it and I would say, 'Take it away from me before I break it.'"

And so he showed me that within this outwardly chipper youngster there is a great murderous rage.

I told Rick that since I was eight I had had many fears; I was afraid of the dark, and of crabs and lobsters. Although I had once been bitten on the toe by a crab, what really scared me was that I had heard that a lobster could bite your finger off. I had nightmares that lobsters or crabs were coming to get me.

I was also claustrophobic. I couldn't stand to be in an elevator; I used to walk up sixteen flights to get to my home.

And I was terrified of being lost. I couldn't explore new trails on my bike, like my friends did, because I worried that I would not be able to find my way back. And even at twelve I would start to feel faint and frantic if I became separated from my mother.

I noticed that Jeffrey has a serious tic in both eyes and brought this to his attention. He claimed that it was caused by the track lights, so I turned them off. The tic continued. I interpreted that perhaps there was something he did not want to "see" in the psychological sense, and that this was translated into a real "not seeing" by the tic.

After the next session, Rick drove me home again. I didn't feel too comfortable in the car; I felt trapped. I didn't feel that I could get out, and, especially at that time, I always liked to plan my next move in case something happened. When we arrived in front of my house I was in a hurry to get out; I tried to pull the latch to open the door. It didn't open. My heart started to beat fast and I pulled many times on the door latch. Rick said, "Wait, Jeffrey, wait. I have to open the door lock. They all open and lock from the driver's door."

And I replied, "That's a great idea if you wanted to sexually abuse a child; he wouldn't be able to get out."

At the beginning of the next session we were just kidding around when Rick said, "Fuck," rather lightheartedly. He looked up as if surprised to hear the word and said, "Who said that? It must have been me; you're too nice."

I said, "I'm not that nice."

And he asked, "Does that mean not nice on the inside, but nice on the outside?"

And then suddenly for no reason I totally forgot the question.

Rick repeated the question to me, and I replied, "I'm *not* nice around grown-ups . . . I mean, I *am* nice around grown-ups."

Rick laughed and explained that when we say what we mean and it turns out not to be what we intended to say it can help us to understand our real feelings.

I had the feeling that Jeffrey was overly moral and hard on himself so I asked him if it would be all right to read him a fairy tale. He seemed surprised but agreed, and so I read him about half of Andersen's "The Garden of Paradise."[4] I hoped by the end that he would see that we are all human and flawed.

At the next session we finished the fairy tale. Jeffrey had a good feeling of what it was about and a discussion of human weakness did follow. Since I had read to him, I thought to ask him what bedtime rituals had been like for him as a young child. He replied that he couldn't remember being read to, but he always had company at night. First he shared a room with his sister, and then his brother moved in and the sister took the brother's room for her

---

[4]For those who are not familiar with this charming, if lesser known, tale of Andersen's, it revolves around an initially arrogant prince who feels that if he had been in Adam's place we would all still be in Paradise. He is given the chance and loses the Garden in just one day. It is worth reading this story for Andersen's description of the Garden alone.

own. And, he added, his father also sleeps in the room with him in a bunk bed that his father built! How the most innocent question leads us deep into the forest. Jeffrey told me that the parents have not slept in the same room for years! He offered as an explanation that his father's religious belief was (Jeffrey thought) that married people should not sleep together (i.e., have sex) unless they are trying to have a child.

On weekends when I slept over at my friend's house I would be terrified at not knowing where my parents were. The next morning I would feel sick to my stomach with worry; I would call my house to talk with them, but often they had already left for work. I would try everything to get in touch with them and I would not stop feeling sick until I did. I talked to myself to try to convince myself that everything was all right and that I had nothing to worry about. I used to get so frustrated that I would become all tense inside and say to myself, "Why are you doing this? What's the point?"

When someone wasn't home, I would listen for the sound of the elevator opening, hoping that it was someone, anyone. When someone didn't come back on time I always used to feel that I had to do something to waste time, like go out to the store, so that they would have extra time in which to come home. If they didn't come home in that extra time, I'd be twice as scared. I'd panic; everything seemed to be going through my head at once. I'd think, "This has happened," or "That has happened," and "I'll never see them again. Who will take care of me?"

I used to stay up at night and wait for my mother to come home from school board meetings. Often that was as late as two in the morning, and then I would have trouble getting up for school. My grades dropped some during this period. I would worry about whether my parents would be home when they were supposed to be, and that would make me sick in school so that I wanted to go home.

All I ever cared about was my family and my house. I told Rick, "My house is a symbol of where everything happens." I didn't know how much longer I could go on like that.

It became increasingly clear to me that Jeffrey felt that his worrying, in some way, might serve to control the family, perhaps to force them to stay together. But the more intriguing question was why he was so obsessed with having this kind of control. Of course, the parental fights (and the father's physical abandonment—emotional, too?—of the mother in moving into the boys' room) had frightened him, as they would any child, and he might just be trying to prevent a divorce. But the reaction seemed so extreme. I was lost, but we went on.

On the way home somehow the conversation turned to sex. I asked Jeffrey some rather innocuous question but got no answer. I turned to look at him and saw a somewhat enigmatic smile and so I said, "I guess you don't want to talk about this, right?" He said that that was so, so I dropped it, but said that I thought we might discuss it at our next session.

The following week, when the subject of sex came up again, Jeffrey at first seemed very relaxed, but burst into

*tears as soon as he opened his mouth. He pleaded with me
to change the subject, and I said that it was OK, but we
should talk about why we could not talk about sex. He
confided that his parents would disapprove of him if they
knew about his sex life, and since I also was a grown-up, I
was also likely to disapprove. I thought perhaps he was
talking about masturbation, as his father is not likely to
approve of such an activity, and I already knew how his
older brother felt about it (very negatively). I assured him
that I would not disapprove of him.*

*Toward the end of the session Jeffrey asked me about
my sex life at his age. I answered as candidly as possible,
and he seemed greatly relieved.*

*On the way home I asked how much he hated my
bringing up the subject of sex, and he replied that on a
scale from one to ten, he hated it eight and a half.*

I was very uncomfortable at the next session, though I
didn't know why. Rick brought up the subject of sex
again, but I didn't think there was any need to talk about
it. I told him so and then I was going to explain something
else to him. But when I opened my mouth I suddenly burst
into tears. Rick asked me why I was crying, but I could
only shake my head from left to right, indicating that I
didn't know myself; Rick asked me if it had to do with
masturbation. I said, "No. It's just that if my parents knew
about my thoughts about sex they wouldn't approve of
them." Rick hugged me and said, "Let's change the subject."

After a few minutes I stopped crying and we talked
about other things, but at the end of the session the subject
came back to sex again. I asked Rick what his sex life had

been like at my age. It was my way of changing the subject of sex off of me and onto Rick. He told me briefly about it and I felt very relieved. It also made me feel much more comfortable about the whole subject because I saw that he didn't feel uncomfortable and also that I wasn't doing anything abnormal.

So I told him that I masturbated, too, and we talked about that for a little while.

During the week after that session I knew that there was something very important that I had to tell Rick. I hadn't told him up to that point because I didn't see any connection between it and the problems that had brought me to therapy. But somehow I knew that in discussing sex it would come out. Somehow I felt that Rick already knew and was just waiting for me to tell him.

I was sexually abused when I was six.

I thought about how I could bring myself to say it in words. On the way over to Rick's office I nearly went crazy on the bus thinking about how I would tell him, saying the words to myself and pretending to be him and imagining his reaction. I didn't know whether I should just come out and say it, but I didn't see how I could bring it up any other way. I wasn't even sure that I would be able to say it. I began to feel faint.

But when I walked into Rick's office, it was the first thing that I said.

As soon as Jeffrey came in he said, sitting down on the couch, "I have something to tell you. I've never told any-

one before. I was sexually abused." He started to cry and developed a severe left-sided headache.

I replied, "I know, Jeffrey, I know."

He did not seem that surprised, but he asked how I knew, and I led him through my thinking, confiding that I had thought that perhaps he was involved with either his older brother or his father. He did not seem shocked at this but denied ever having any sexual contact with either of them.

He told me that he had been abused by a friend of his brother's, named Mark, who at the age of fifteen (when Jeffrey was six) had asked Jeffrey over to his house. When Jeffrey arrived and called out, Mark replied that he was in the bathroom and that Jeffrey should come in. Jeffrey did and discovered Mark naked. Mark then closed (possibly locked) the bathroom door and asked Jeffrey to suck on his penis.

"I did for about fifteen minutes, and then he told me to stop. He told me not to tell anyone."

Jeffrey knew that they had done something wrong but did not know that he had been abused. So he told no one.

By age nine, however, he learned that there are homosexuals and heterosexuals and assumed that he was homosexual because:

1. He was the cocksucker (his term), and

2. He hadn't resisted or put up a fight.

Even currently, when he is attracted to a girl and goes after her, he feels that he shouldn't be doing it because he is a homosexual.

I tried to counter as much of these distortions as possible, as well as suggesting that he would have to decide how to discharge his rage at Mark (whom he clearly would like to kill); Mark lives nearby and thus is still available. Perhaps I would go there with Jeffrey if he had the strength.

Interestingly, he told me that Mark lost his mother when he was seven, and recently lost his father and grandmother. He said that Mark was a really harmless (?!) boy.

"If you would see him, you would never believe that he could do something like that."

I suggested that Jeffrey was trying to excuse Mark by understanding him but that understanding why a person did something was not the same as excusing what they did. I did not want Jeffrey to water down his rage and keep it internalized where it would destroy him.

He said that he didn't feel that he could face Mark and asked how it would help.

I tried to make him see, but I knew that he was not ready. It was clear why he would not tell his parents — he believed that everyone would say that he was the homosexual for the same reasons he had told himself. It is also clear why he shies away so from affection.

On the way out of the office we stopped at the cheese store; I got some cheese, and Jeffrey asked for some fudge, which I bought for him — a little something sweet after such bitterness! When we got to his house, I thanked him once again for trusting me and praised him again for his bravery.

I wept on the way home.

I was over at my brother's friend Mark's house. They were playing with Mark's trains and I was watching. When we were ready to go home, Mark said that it would be all right if I came up there whenever I wanted to play with the trains. That really appealed to me. It made me really happy. I felt that then I would have the trains all to myself.

The next day, I think, I got the urge to go over and play with the trains since now I knew that they were there for me and that it was OK. I walked up the street to Mark's house. I was very excited when I arrived. I knocked on the door and called his name. There was no answer, so, not thinking, I opened the door and went in. I called his name again. Again there was no answer.

It was a cloudy day and sort of dark out. I saw a light in the bathroom. I went right up next to the door and said, "Mark?"

And he said, "Yeh. Jeffrey, come on in. The door's open."

I opened the door and saw Mark standing naked in the shower trying to fix the shower curtain which appeared stuck. The water was just running a little bit. I don't think he had taken a shower yet.

He stepped out of the bathtub and walked right past me and closed the door. Then he turned around, stepped toward me, leaned back against the sink and said, "Suck it." Remembering back, I know now that he was almost fully erect when he asked me to do it.

I sucked on it for about ten or fifteen minutes. He kept looking down at me, then closing his eyes, then looking down at me again. He had a funny expression on his face; I thought he was in pain.

Finally, he said, "Stop." He opened the bathroom door and stepped out and said, "Don't tell *anybody*."

I left the bathroom. It seemed even darker in the room because the light was on in the bathroom. Mark was not around. I left and went home.

A few days later I saw Mark sitting on his doorstep smoking a cigarette. I rode up to him on my bicycle and confided that I had not told anybody. But he just ignored me.

And so, until I told Rick, I never told anybody else.

Twenty minutes or so before the next session, Jeffrey called to tell me that he didn't think he would be coming because of severe gas pains. He claimed that he had had them, on and off, for the last two days, ever since he ate an eclair (shape? filled with cream?). He told me that he had left the house with his mother on his way to see me but had had an attack and returned.

"So," he said rather quickly, "I'll see you next week."

I replied that I thought he should come anyhow unless he was really very sick as it seemed likely that the pain, at this late date, was psychosomatic. Jeffrey seemed almost relieved to hear me say that and promptly said that he was on his way. No argument at all.

During the session I read my notes from last week to Jeffrey. At the end he cried because he did not feel that he could face Mark. I assured him that he would be able to some day and that I would go with him.

He seemed surprised and asked, "You mean physically go?" and when I replied affirmatively, he said, "But if he saw me coming with you that would give away the whole thing." I replied that when the time came we would not make a surprise visit but rather would prearrange it with Mark.

Then Jeffrey brought up some of his vindictive fantasies regarding Mark. The main one he has had many times (the others are listed in the chapter appendix). "I keep seeing him running naked from his house. I lift my double-

barreled (shape!) shotgun and aim and shoot him right in the chest."

I interpreted the nakedness as Jeffrey making Mark as totally vulnerable and defenseless as he, Jeffrey, had been when the tables had been turned. Jeffrey said that after he killed Mark he would just go to jail for two years because he is a minor; clearly he had thought quite seriously about committing this murder. I suggested that confronting Mark verbally would be better because then Jeffrey would not be punished (by going to jail) for venting his justified rage at this boy who has caused him so much suffering.

God how I ache for him.

When I arrived at Rick's I felt better. We talked for about ten minutes trying to figure out what had made me sick; Rick thought that it might have been psychosomatic. I automatically thought that he was wrong because I couldn't imagine that you could become so sick just because you didn't want to do something. I thought about how nervous I felt when I had to take tests in school, but I couldn't believe that you could feel as sick as I had felt. So Rick dropped the whole subject.

Then Rick read me his notes from the last session, and we talked about getting together with Mark. That came as a shock to me because the last thing I wanted to do was to see Mark. I didn't think that could help, just make it worse for me because then I would be reminded of it. Rick explained why he thought it would help, but I didn't even consider it.

I told Rick about my fantasies about hurting Mark. He asked me to explain why I would do each one of them and tried to explain how they would only get me into more trouble. I didn't care because the only thing I cared about was getting back at him. I thought that I could stand the consequences, even if it was going to jail, just to have the satisfaction of making Mark suffer.

The revelation of Jeffrey's abuse radically changed the entire focus of therapy. His obsessive worrying, while still quite a problem, was put aside.

Jeffrey's agony in revealing what had occurred was dramatically somaticized in the moments immediately after he told me. He grabbed his head as if he had been stabbed in the left temporal lobe.

I felt it too. The experience of a personal psychoanalysis, I think, allows the analyst to feel the depth of trust which precedes such disclosures. All the terror that accompanies them—that the analyst will now hate us as we hate ourselves, will reject us, will think us sick, disgusting, hopeless—must be overcome. It is the personal experience of these fears, and their neurotic foundations, which helps the analyst to understand, to accept, and to grasp this potentially most destructive moment and turn it into a triumph of human love.

In the next few sessions Jeffrey went over the details of his abuse, talking of his brother's friend and their lives together up until that final day. He talked of his scattered sexual interests and attempts (all heterosexual) since that

117

time and more in depth of his confusion and guilt when with a girl.

But over and over he came back to the scene. The bathroom door was open when he walked in. Mark had walked over to it and closed it (but had he locked it?) before he told Jeffrey what to do. Over and over again Jeffrey was tormented by his doubts. If the door wasn't locked then why hadn't he tried to escape? Because he wanted it to happen? Because he was a homosexual? But he couldn't remember if Mark had locked it or not and tortured himself with his uncertainty. And so all my assurances (e.g., "You wouldn't have wanted that because a six-year-old doesn't know about such sexual activities.") fell on doubting and deaf ears. I asked Jeffrey to describe the physical layout of the bathroom to me and I sketched it out on paper while he did. It looked like this:

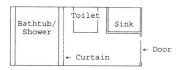

As nearly as I could follow it Mark's path was as shown below:

The connection between Jeffrey's presenting symptoms and his sexual abuse came to me at last. When Mark had closed the door, Jeffrey was suddenly cut off from the outside world, alone, helpless, and out of control.

Jeffrey N.

Now, if he did not have control over when his parents were home his feelings of helplessness and isolation reawakened the terror of impending disaster. Not just an expectable effort to keep what he perceived as a disintegrating family together, it obtained its obsessive character because of his fear that he would be alone again, helpless again, left to be abused again.

No wonder he never entered an elevator by himself! Oh God, to be alone in a closed place when the door closed, its opening beyond his control. And the horror of seeing the man shot in the park, reinforcing his own hidden knowledge of the abrupt and evil twists that life can take (to say nothing of the more subtle Freudian symbolism of the shooting pistol and its destructiveness).

And I suddenly realized that the bathroom adjoining my waiting room (with a little imagination) was extremely close in design to Jeffrey's personal, fateful one. It looks like this:

If I closed the bathroom door and imagined that wall was solid and that the shower door was now the bathroom door, I could easily see this and I hope that the reader can as well.

And I knew, if I could convince Jeffrey, what we had to do in our next session.

After our initial work in the next session, I pointed out to Jeffrey the similarities in the two bathrooms by drawing it out for him. And then I asked him if we could go up to the bathroom and walk through what had happened between Mark and himself. He said, "Sure," in a strong voice, but we walked upstairs together slowly.

Once in the bathroom I closed the door and explained again that that wall was now solid and the shower door was now substituting for the bathroom door.

Then I said that I would be Mark and that he should tell me what to do. Carefully he detailed my actions and I followed his instructions slowly, step by step. At the point where I reached and closed the door, leaned back against the sink and door, and repeated Mark's words ("Suck on it") I knew what I had wanted to find out. I was positioned between Jeffrey and the closed door. Locked or unlocked, there was no way that he could have escaped; no way he, at six, could possibly have moved a fifteen-year-old. I held my knowledge to myself though, wary of being cheated by any fluke of memory.

Instead, I said to Jeffrey, "Can we walk through this just one more time?" He agreed and I asked him to close his eyes while he gave me instructions to make sure that we were reenacting the events exactly as they had occurred. He repeated it all exactly as the first time, if a little more slowly, more considered this time. But, nonetheless, I wound up exactly where I had been before. And the die was cast.

"Where am I?" I asked.

Jeffrey looked bewildered and answered, "In front of me, just like Mark was."

"But where am I in terms of you and the door?"

Jeffrey N.

"You're between me and the door."

"Exactly, Jeffrey, and there's no way you can get past me and through the door. It's closed. Bathroom doors open in. Turning the knob wouldn't help. But most of all, Jeffrey, it doesn't make any difference whether or not the door was locked. You couldn't get out anyway."

Jeffrey stared at me as it sank in. So I repeated myself. "You can't get by me Jeff. It doesn't make any difference whether I lock the door or not."

At last it reached him. I reached out for him and held him, opened the door and we stepped out.

"You were really brave to go in there with me," I said. "I can't believe you really did it."

"Neither can I."

When Rick asked me to reenact what had happened between Mark and me, I was scared and confused. I didn't understand why we were going to go in there (Rick's bathroom); it seemed that everything Rick said we should do, I didn't want to do. But I went anyhow, partly because I didn't want to seem scared and partly because I didn't want to disappoint Rick.

I was shitting bricks all the way up the stairs to the bathroom. We went in and Rick closed the door. I didn't feel any more frightened when he closed the door because I don't think that you can feel more frightened than I already was.

After we acted through what had happened, Rick pointed out how I couldn't have gotten out of the bathroom and away from Mark. Knowing that didn't help very much at the time, but it helped a lot later on. We left the bathroom and Rick congratulated me for being brave enough to go into the bathroom with another man.

I couldn't believe that I had done it, but I did feel very brave.

The second year of therapy seemed to fly by. Jeffrey continued to improve. There were fewer incidents at home, and, happily, his parents' relationship seemed quieter, more stable. We talked often of contacting Mark, but for a long time Jeffrey was set on vengeance.

I argued that all of his plans would only, ultimately, wind up with his being punished as well. I asked if he didn't think he had already been punished enough. I told him, over and over, that a confrontation would help him, allow him to vent his anger, allow him to hurt Mark with the truth. And, of course, there was the hope of an apology. Then, maybe, there could be healing, quiet.

And yet, even though I felt that this was the only satisfaction he could ever have, Jeffrey made me clearly see how thin the fabric of our civilized society is; I knew the depth of his rage, and, quite candidly, I also felt revenge would bring him greater satisfaction. I felt that the alternative I had offered was so very, very little and weak. But what could ever balance out his torment, his years of suffering? I don't know and will never know.

Finally, toward the end of the second year, Jeffrey felt ready. I searched for Mark and found that he had married and moved. I left a message and he returned it while I was in a session. He seemed quite anxious; even before he knew that I was Jeffrey's analyst, or even what the call was about, he asked if he had herpes or AIDS(!). I said that was not what this call was about and arranged to call him back.

I called back with Jeffrey listening in. Mark acknowl-

*edged that he knew the family and Jeffrey well. But he
affected shock and disbelief at what Jeffrey had told me
and flatly denied it.*

*I wrote a letter to Mark and encouraged him to be
honest with Jeffrey, to apologize, to allow Jeffrey to bury
the past. There was no reply.*

*Jeffrey decided that he would call and I would listen.
It turned out to be a good decision. Mark initially denied
the whole thing, as he had to me, but Jeffrey stood his
ground. He challenged Mark, who then fell back on memory loss. But Jeffrey kept pushing him, and finally Mark
began to backwater, offering that perhaps the incident had
only been inoffensively sexual ("Maybe [you saw me]
masturbating") or perhaps that he had been drunk. Trying
to excuse himself to Jeffrey and me, he said that maybe he
had been drunk and told Jeffrey that he had also been
taking his father's drugs at that time ("Did you tell your
doctor that?" [How would Jeffrey have known?]).*

*Mark asked worriedly if Jeffrey thinks of this often
and Jeffrey told him what suffering this has brought to
him. Mark repeated that he didn't want Jeff to think about
this all the time because he didn't want Jeff to be "fucked
up"; but he fell short of an honest admission. Jeff hung up.*

Rick suggested that I confront Mark if we could find
out where he lived. I found out his old telephone number
from Long Island, but when Rick called he found out that
Mark had married and moved to Oklahoma. Rick got
Mark's new number from Mark's old employer and called
him up.

I wanted to listen in, so Rick called me up at home and
secretly I listened to Rick and Mark's conversation. It was

hard not saying a word while Mark denied the whole thing, but I kept my mouth shut. We listened to the tape together at my next session; I wasn't surprised that Mark had denied it.

Rick and I discussed what to do next and Rick suggested writing a letter to Mark (see chapter appendix).

We never got a response to that letter and so we decided to call again. This time I called and Rick listened.

Mark asked whether I was at Rick's office. I lied and said that I was at home; I thought he might be more honest if he thought it was just me on the phone.

He seemed to know what the phone call was about and asked the first question. "Now what is this story that you told the doctor about my molesting you?"

I replied, "Didn't that happen?" and Mark denied it. Then he didn't really deny it; he said that he didn't remember anything like that happening, and was worried that "You [will] go through life thinking you're fucked up."

Then he said that maybe I had walked into the bathroom and seen him masturbating. He said that it was years and years ago and he really didn't remember.

I asked Mark if maybe he had been drunk, because my older brother had told me that Mark drank heavily as a teenager. He replied that maybe he had been, and that he had also been taking his father's pills at the time.

I really wanted him to just come out and say that it had happened, and to some extent he did by continuously modifying his story. But I didn't care what his cover was; I just wanted him to admit that it had happened.

He said I could call him whenever I wanted to. I hung up.

Jeffrey N.

It has been over a year since Jeffrey and I made those telephone calls to Mark. Somehow, in our last full year of therapy the issue of re-contacting Mark never seemed to have the urgency for Jeffrey that it did during the second year. I guess that it has always been in the back of my mind; perhaps I think that it would somehow be better if Mark actually came to New York, admitted the truth to Jeffrey, and apologized. I don't know. The urgency doesn't seem to exist in me anymore either.

What has emerged as the central theme in our last year together is the development of trust. What never ending hope there is in children! How can I convey the enormity of the gift a child gives when he gives us his trust? Especially when he has trusted and been hurt before. It is so great that no gift we can give back is adequate. Committing yourself to be there always for a child is, after all, a conscious choice; each time I do it I know what I am offering—the sacrifices that will be asked of me, how it will limit my freedom.

But the child who gives me his trust is making a leap of faith. He is saying that even though he has been hurt before, he will trust this one more time, throw himself out to me, daring, hoping, trusting that I will be there to catch him, as promised.

Jeffrey's first major leap of faith was telling me about his abuse. Then, there was his bravery in reenacting the scene of his abuse with me.

But finally, Jeffrey's ultimate gift of trust was incredible even to me. So great and yet so simple, so human.

Jeffrey's neurotic difficulties had come to an end. His tics had disappeared, as had his claustrophobia. As he became increasingly less fearful of losing his parents, he became more involved in adventures with his friends. He started riding a dirt bike, traveling miles from his house. As his need to control everything and everyone else diminished, he became freer, happier. His sense of humor emerged. He laughed and joked. What a miracle! Our sessions became the casual, honest give-and-take of two friends. He started actively pursuing girls. He became a boy again, alive again.

And then, at the end of a session, having already opened the door (just in case ?!), Jeffrey reached up, pulled my neck down and kissed me.

When I first came to Rick, I don't think I understood trust. Sure, you trusted a friend but not in the same way because you keep certain things away from them because you might be rejected. In Rick's case, not everything was approved of, but everything was accepted.

I thought that all of our meetings would be like the first few, but they weren't. During the course of time a certain amount of trust built up between Rick and me. The way I first built up some trust was by testing Rick with little bits of information to see how (and if) he would accept them.

My tests of Rick built a ladder for me to climb on, slowly pulling one foot at a time up this ladder of trust. This ladder was composed of his reactions to different situations that I found and fed to him, carefully grading him like a teacher grades a student. Rick came out with all A's, but the question was, could I feed him the ultimate question? Being rejected was my greatest fear. I tried to play out his reaction in my mind and study it, but I couldn't see his reaction. Taking the last step to the top of the ladder was scary. I was so confused that I didn't know how to tell him.

Then, before one meeting, with little preparation I hit Rick with everything I had. I told him that when I was six I was sexually abused. Like I hoped, Rick accepted it; he said we could cope with it, he didn't blame me, he understood it. I still hadn't been sure that he would when I told him. But after I told him, I realized that he was the only person I could have told. I had begun to really trust him.

Now that I knew that I could trust him with my deepest secret, coping with the problem became less impossible. Reenacting and talking about it would bring me closer to overcoming my terror of facing Mark and facing my rage.

My fear of reenacting the scene of my abuse was almost as great as the abuse itself. So when Rick suggested that we do just that, I suddenly felt nauseous and light-headed.

Rick asked me if I thought I could do it, and I said yes.

But saying yes was easier than walking up the stairs to the bathroom knowing that I would be trapped in a room with a much older person; that I would be in the same situation I had been in before. Realizing that I was walking into it again, of my own free will, but walking into it again nevertheless, I felt the greatest fear I had ever felt. I thought I would faint. The fear was so great that it matched the fear I felt in the bathroom when I heard the door close.

I knew all the way up that I didn't have to go through with it. I also knew that there were two things that could happen—Rick could take advantage of me, or he could just do what he said he was going to. I decided to trust him and, in doing so, gave him the perfect opportunity to abuse me. If he didn't do it then, he would never do it.

After I knew I could trust Rick to any extent, I became as comfortable with him as I am with myself. Kissing him became my way of saying hello and goodbye. After all I had been through with him, it was the only way I could show my love for him. And it allowed him to show his love for me back.

I am writing this part of this chapter several months after therapy has come to an end. Rick and I agreed at the end of last school year that we could stop our weekly sessions. All the difficulties that I had had when I originally came to see Rick have long since disappeared. I am no longer claustrophobic, and I have no trouble exploring places distant from my home without fearing being lost. I no longer have my tics.

But best of all I no longer think that I am gay. I know that it was all Mark's fault; I am fifteen now, and since I don't worry that I shouldn't like girls because I am gay, I find myself going out with them more and more, responding sexually to them more and more.

Knowing that what happened is in the past and does not affect me now, I can go on with my life. I feel brave and independent again. My world is full of fun and adventure again. I feel happy and free.

JEFFREY'S FANTASIES

1. Hanging Mark by his penis.
2. Hanging Mark by his teeth.
3. Blackmail and extortion. I would be in control; he would be sitting in a chair; he'd be listening and I'd say, "If you don't give me two hundred dollars a week, I'll send you to prison for years."
4. Stringing up notes. I would string up notes on his front door. They would say, "REMEMBER ME, ASSHOLE?" one week and, "YOU FAGGOT FUCK, YOU'RE DEAD MEAT," the next week. The third week they would say, "YOU STUPID FAGGOT, I WAS ONLY SIX YEARS OLD." I would stick a note in his girlfriend's car; it would say, "YOUR BOYFRIEND RAPED A SIX YEAR OLD KID."
5. I would sabotage his truck. I would loosen up the bolts on his wheels and set up spikes under his seat.
6. I would go into his bathroom and spray-paint FAGGOT on the shower curtain.
7. I'd film his reactions to what he saw.
8. I'd put a big hole in his floor and put a carpet over it. When he fell through I would hit him with bricks.
9. I'd go into his house and put a pack of cigarettes there which had cyanide powder in them. When he smoked one he would inhale the gas and suffer extreme pain and internal injuries.
10. I would put up a fake penis on the first wall he would see when he came in the door of his house. It would have an axe through it. There would be a note under it saying, "REMEMBER ME, YOU FAGGOT?"
11. I would bend all his knives and forks and spoons.
12. I'd put up a half-poster size picture of a baby. The baby

would be naked. All over it would be written, "LOOK FA-MILIAR?"

13. I would take out the screws on his refrigerator door, and when he would open it the heavy door would fall on his foot.

FIRST PHONE CALL

Rick: I'll tell you why I wanted to get in touch with you, Mark. I have a patient who I've had for about two years now in the city. His name is Jeffrey N.

Mark: Uh huh.

R: And, uh Jeffrey, uh, about a year and a half ago, uh, told me about something that happened between you and him a very long time ago.

M: Jeffrey?

R: Yeah.

M: Little Jeffrey?

R: Little Jeffrey.

M: Okay. What did he say what happened?

R: Well, according to Jeffrey when he was about six or possibly seven years old when you would have been about fifteen, I would imagine this was about seven years ago, I don't know how old you are now . . .

M: Oh, I knew Jeffrey since he was little . . . I was friends with Dave and Sue and Paul and everybody. I know the whole family very well.

R: Yeah, no. Jeffrey has told me that. Well, about a year and a half ago Jeffrey told me that when he was about six or seven he went over to your house out on the Island and, uh, you were coming out of the shower and you asked him to come in the bathroom, and in the bathroom there was a, an episode of what would pass nowadays for sexual molestation between you and him.

Jeffrey N.

M: He told you that?

R: Yep.

M: Well I . . . Doctor! You're accusing me of child molesting, or whatever you call it.

R: I'm not accusing you of anything.

M: OK. . . .

R: I'm telling you that . . .

M: Well it's disturbing to me that he would say that.

R: Well, see the thing is this—the original problems that Jeffrey was sent to me for did not make very much sense until after I'd been seeing him for a couple of months and when he told me about this incident which is, I assure you, quite real in his mind if not real in yours, everything that has gone wrong in his life since then made a great deal of sense. In any case, at the time, which was, as I said, about a year and a half ago, we discussed at some length his feelings about what he recalls as well as his feelings about you, since he recalls you being involved in it. And what we eventually settled on after about a year was that when he felt ready to speak to you that we would call you up and ask you to come here to my office so that the three of us could talk. Unfortunately, just at the point where Jeffrey has felt really comfortable with that idea and comfortable with seeing you, he discovered that you had gotten married and moved to Oklahoma. So, here we are on the telephone. And this is why I am calling you.

M: (Silence) Holy Shit. (Nervous laughter) Doctor, I just, . . . I, I, I'm, . . . I don't know what to say, I know how, I know how Jeffrey's had problems in the past, but, I mean, you're a psychologist . . .

R: I'm a psychoanalyst.

M: Psychoanalyst, oh, OK. (Short pause) Well doctor, I, I don't know what to tell you. I don't know what to tell you. Because, I mean, I never in my life have ever done anything like that and I don't remember that happening. I do not remember this happening. Now whether Jeffrey has, is blocking something in his own head or you know, I just, I just cannot imagine myself doing this and ever, . . . it never happened! That never happened. I remember, . . . the only time Jeffrey ever came to my house was with Dave.

R: Well the incident that Jeffrey recalls, it basically runs like this, is that, in fact he didn't go with Dave. It was, he came over on an afternoon, as I said, you were in a bathroom in the house and he called out your name and you said come in and came out from the shower apparently naked, I'm just giving you the capsule of this, walked past Jeffrey, closed the bathroom door and told him to fellate you, which is medicalese for give you a blow job. As I said he was about seven then, you would have been about fifteen.

M: (Sighs) Oh my God.

R: You know, I don't think it would be likely that you would have forgotten something like that if it happened.

M: Sure, nothing like that ever happened. You better talk to Jeffrey, 'cause this is blowing my mind. I cannot, first of all I've never been attracted to guys, second I, I . . . (Pause, sigh)

R: Now you have to understand something Mark, you're not being accused of anything, I'm not a lawyer and I'm not the New York City prosecutor.

M: Oh, I understand that, you know, I mean what are we, you know I've, I've seen a couple of psychoanalysts myself, but, you know, I mean, I'll tell you one thing is I'm not a liar and if the kid's going to have this problem the whole life, you know, if something like this did happen I'd come in and talk to you, but I just can't understand why, you know, young Jeffrey would say something like that when . . . if something like this did happen I would remember it. I'm positive I would. I should hope I would.

R: Well, I don't know, he . . .

Jeffrey N.

M: That's also six years ago, you know, but I, I . . .

R: He forgot about it for a long time himself, apparently because it was very painful, but the effect . . .

M: What does Sue think about this?

R: Nobody knows about this. The . . . I'm the only person who knows about this and for I think very obvious reasons it's not the kind of thing that a boy runs home and tells his parents.

M: (Pause) You . . .

R: Is it? . . .

. . . I would venture so far as to say it seems quite clear to me that at more or less the time he's talking about, somebody sexually molested Jeffrey and in very much the way he says, because the effects are much too real and the difficulties are much too real. Obviously, you know, since he says it was you, that's why I'm looking for you; and obviously at this point in his life Jeffrey realizes that if you would say yes this did happen, that the only satisfaction he can have is in fact to talk to you and to say, hey, this happened and this hurt me and you know, to straighten it away in his own head. I mean, we're talking about something that happened many years ago.

M: I understand that. But (sigh) . . . fuckin' Jeffrey. Man, what the fuck is with him?

R: Well, I'll be . . . I will of course relay this entire phone conversation to him, but you know I want you to be aware of the fact that [the] only reason I did not make any attempt to contact you earlier is because Jeffrey didn't feel comfortable with it. I think that when this came back to his mind and when he first confronted this he was just furious, and that has taken quite a bit of time to put away. Nobody is looking to prosecute you or drag you back to New York on a child abuse . . .

M: I can remember Jeffrey going up in the woods with his buddies and playing doctor or whatever, but, uh, you know, there is a woods right a block from my house, but nothing like this doctor, you know, I mean, that's, it's a fucking crime man.

R: Yeah, I know, but of course when he was seven and you were fifteen it wouldn't be the same kind of crime as it would be if he'd been seven and you'd been twenty-two. Fifteen-year-old boys do a lot of impulsive things when they have hard-ons you know, that they oughtn't to do, including with girls.

M: Well, doctor, you talk to Jeffrey. . . . When's his next appointment?

R: Well, I'll be seeing him tomorrow. But I assume, that being as you're a married person, you're reachable at this number. . . .

M: Yes sir.

R: And I will probably be getting back to you.

M: OK.

R: All right?

M: Yes sir.

R: OK. Thank you very much for your time.

M: Yep. Bye bye.

R: Bye bye.

LETTER TO MARK

Frederick H. Berenstein
177 East 79th Street
New York, New York 10021

May x, xxxx

Mr. Mark X.
xxxxxxxxxxx
xxxxxxxxxxx

Dear Mr. X,

I am writing to you as a follow-up to our telephone conversation last week. As I told you then, I am Jeffrey N.'s psychoanalyst; I am not a police officer, nor a detective, nor an attorney. My only concern is for Jeffrey's well-being.

Jeffrey, as I also told you, revealed to me almost a year and a half ago that he had been sexually molested when he was about seven years old; at that time, and to this date, Jeffrey has always maintained that you were the person who molested him. I felt then, and I still feel now, that Jeffrey's suffering could really be helped if the three of us met together. After all, what other satisfaction can Jeffrey have but that one. I did not contact you immediately simply because I had to wait until Jeffrey became comfortable with the idea.

After so many years it may seem to you that this whole affair is simply Jeffrey's word against yours, but it is not. Jeffrey has submitted to scientifically monitored lie detection about this incident; *he is telling the truth*. On the telephone you said that if such an incident had happened you would, of course, come in to talk with Jeffrey and myself. Although I know how difficult it must be for you, I must urge you to swallow your embarrassment and shame, to admit to this incident which happened so long ago (and about which no people other than myself and Jeffrey know), and to come back to New York to help Jeffrey in the only way you can.

I am anxiously awaiting your reply.

Sincerely,

Frederick Berenstein

SECOND PHONE CALL

(Sound of dial tone, phone being dialed and phone ringing)

Jeffrey: (Sighs)

Mark: Hello.

J: Hello, is Mark there?

M: Oh yeah, right here.

J: Uh Mark, this is Jeffrey.

M: Heh Jeffrey, what's up?

J: How you doin'?

M: All right. Heh, what's with, uh, the doctor there? What's, what's goin' on with that guy?

J: Oh my doctor?

M: Yeah.

J: Oh, well uh, I've been seeing him for about uh, two years.

M: You know what he says happened? You know, something like that, if that happened Jeffrey, I'm kinda worried about this. If something like that really happened I'd remember it. Now you might have walked in the bathroom and caught me doing somethin' . . . but, uh, you know, is this what you called me about?

J: Well, yeah, just somethin' like that just to, you know (clears throat), just to have a talk, you know.

M: Yeah, OK, OK, 'cause I mean, you know I don't, I don't think there's anything for you to be worried about, don't think about that 'cause that's not, you know, I think maybe, you know, I don't remember but you might have walked in the bathroom and I might have [been] masturbating or something like that.

J: No well, you know, but didn't, didn't that happen.

M: No . . .

J: Don't you remember when I was six or seven, didn't that happen?

M: Uh . . . (sigh). Jeffrey, I don't remember.

J: You don't remember?

M: That was years and years ago, man, I can't . . . I don't remember anything like that ever happening.

J: Hmm . . . well, you know . . .

M: And the doctor said that you told, you told him that uh, the doctor said you told him you gave me a blow job. Now that's crazy Jeffrey! Now how would I, I wouldn't let you do that. Come on.

J: Maybe uh, you know . . .

M: I think what happened was over the years, you kinda stretched it out maybe, in your mind . . .

J: No, I don't think that uh, that I would forget something like that or stretch, stretch it out, you know . . .

M: You don't think you're six years old you're . . . you know, Jesus, when you're a six-year-old kid, wh . . . , uh . . . , you know, how can you remember when you're uh, I can't remember hardly when I was five.

J: Well . . . (short laugh). Listen Mark, this is, has been in my mind for a long time now . . .

M: Well how come you never came up and mentioned it to me? By yourself when I was on the Island?

J: Because, man don't you remember the next day, I came up to you and I said I didn't tell anybody? Don't you remember you were smoking a cigarette on your porch?

M: (Silence) How, wh . . . when was this?

J: This was, I think it was the next day. I remember it. I was on my uh, five-speed bicycle.

M: And what did I say?

J: Uh, you didn't say anything. I asked, I um, I went up, I was riding up the hill, up High Street Hill, and I said um, I said I didn't tell anybody. And then uh, you just didn't say anything. (Silence. Jeffrey coughs.)

M: I don't know man, . . . I mean I . . .

J: You know nobody's here to uh, to you know, to do anything you know . . .

M: Yeah, well, no, I, I just don't want, I don't want you to go through life thinking you're fucked up man, because man, because, you know I, I, Jesus I hope, gee I hope I didn't do something like that I . . . you know this doctor says come back to New York and fly back. Now look it, I ain't got the kind of money to fly back to New York, you know and if I can recall something like that, you know I'll be glad to help you but Jesus Christ . . .

J: Yeah well . . .

M: You know, I mean I don't want you . . .

J: Yeah well . . .

M: Jeffrey, you're a good friend of mine, and Dave's . . .

J: I understand.

M: You've been friends for, you know, a long time, and Dave's my good friend and your whole family is, and if you know, if your family ever heard about this I mean, what the hell would they say?

J: No well, I mean, how's my family ever going to find out? We're just, you know, just trying, you know, [to] get it straight . . .

M: I know, get the story straight, sure.

J: (Clears his throat)

M: Sure, I understand it man. I've seen psychologists before but uh, I don't . . . I think and I think and I think about it and I'm like man? . . . You know?

J: Maybe, uh, you had something before you took a shower maybe? That that . . . ,

M: I had . . .

J: . . . maybe, maybe that wouldn't make you remember?

M: (Silence) I . . .

J: Maybe you had something to drink, you know, 'cause you know, that could happen.

M: I drank a lot awful then, you know that . . .

J: Yeah I knew that . . .

Jeffrey N.

M: I was drunk all of the time . . .

J: . . . you had, you had a lot then.

M: Are you at your doctor's office?

J: No, no I'm at the house. Nobody's home.

M: I don't know where you are or not, man. I'd like to talk to your doctor too and get this fuckin' shit straightened out, man.

J: Hmm. Well I missed him this week you know, I see him uh, next week.

M: Jeffrey don't, . . . I don't understand man, . . . I might have been high or I might have been shit-faced.

J: Hmm.

M: You know I was taking my old man's pills and all that kind of shit back then.

J: Yeah, I know.

M: Did you tell your doctor that?

J: Uh, well I told him that, that you had, uh, you know, maybe, uh, been drinking, and uh, you know, that you had a couple of problems then.

M: Yeah, I know. This isn't . . . I mean, do you think about this often Jeffrey? You know I don't wanna, Jesus it makes me feel . . .

J: Well, I had uh, I still have it a little bit, I had a problem with people whenever they left my house that I would feel that they would, uh, you know, get hurt or be killed or something and I was . . .

M: Why would you feel, what has that got to do with . . .

J: It's, it's kind of hard to exp . . . , it, it all relates to that incident.

M: Are you sure?

J: I'm positive.

M: You're positive 'cause the doctor says so.

J: Yes.

M: (Silence) Well how do you know? Th . . . this, I mean you might have just told this doctor this and he might have just, he might have just blown this all out of proportion. You know you're seeing the guy. He's got a decent, mm, uh, flow of cash coming in for you to see you every week and he's you know . . . you know, that's the way I'm looking at it, is this guy might . . .

J: Well, you see, umm, I, I can, I can see how, it's a perfect pathway to see how it exactly fits in together . . . the way I feel the same way as uh . . . , you know, it was a big trauma. You know I couldn't let anybody leave the house, I was, I was sick, you know, I was nervous, I couldn't stand it anymore until I had to come to him.

M: No shit! Jesus Christ I wish I could do something man, um . . .

J: Mmmm.

M: Tell, uh . . .

J: Well, uh, did you get . . .

M: Next time, next time you're at your doctor's office give me a call and I'll talk to . . .

J: Un-huh . . .

M: . . . and I'll talk to him, man, because I, you know I don't want to cause any fucking trouble . . .

J: Yeah, yeah I know. But you know, there's just one thing. Did you get a letter that we wrote to you?

M: Uh, yes I did. He says, come back to New York immediately, and he never left the phone number, that's right. And he says call back, I mean come back to New York immediately and face up to your guilt or swallow your guilt or some kind of shit, I said what kind of . . .

J: No, no it was just, just a reply, anything, a phone call, a letter . . .

M: No there was no . . .

J: . . . any, any sign of anything. Just a reply, that's all we asked for.

Jeffrey N.

M: Well then, what would a reply read? You know this is a lot better off than a reply just talking with you. You know he's telling me all this shit, you know and he's just confusing me, you know, I'm, you should have just called me th-the first time, you should have just said the hell with it, doctor, I'm going to call Mark and find out what the hell happened.

J: Yeah but I wasn't there.

M: Oh, OK. I thought you were there with him.

J: No.

M: Well look Jeffrey, you tell your doctor, OK . . .

J: OK . . .

M: . . . tell him that if he can get a chance to call me, call me, all right. And tell him, I don't even know where the paper is. Tell him to send me a letter with his address and phone number on it.

J: OK.

M: Or you do it, he's got my address there and let's get this shit straightened out because there's no way, he thinks, he thinks that I'm gonna, that I can fly back to New York, now if he wants to pay for it, if he wants to pay for my plane ticket here and there and a hotel room or whatever, sure I'll be glad, you know and time off of work I'll be glad to come but other than that, I mean you know I'm busting my ass here with air conditioning just to pay these, . . . and I don't even have the money to even do that . . .

J: Yeah I know.

M: . . . to pay for travel and shit.

J: No, we'll work something out, OK.

M: OK Jeff, but just think about it. What I think, you know I might have been totally shit-faced off my mind, and you, I think since six years old . . .

J: Yeah . . .

M: . . . it got into your mind and this trauma has built up so bad that maybe it never really happened the way you think.

J: Yeah, well, . . .
M: OK.
J: I have a pretty good idea.
M: OK, Jeff.
J: OK, bye bye.
M: Take it easy.
(Sound of phone hanging up.)
J: Rick.
R: Umm-hmm.

5

ADAM O.

Death in the Afternoon

Though nothing can bring back the hour
Of splendor in the grass, of glory in the flower;
We will grieve not, rather find
Strength in what remains behind.

William Wordsworth
"Intimations of Immortality"

There was never a patient to whom I brought greater pain than Adam. Adam who had it all and lost it all. Adam whose father wasn't supposed to die but died anyhow. Adam who never got to say goodbye. Adam whom I held tight while he faced the unfaceable. Adam whom I loved and wanted for my own.

Adam's father had been terminally ill, but Adam did

not know it. Even at the end, in his last hospitalization, the doctors had assured Mrs. O. that he would survive. On the day his father died, Adam, almost thirteen, was with a relative. His mother spoke to him on the phone and asked if he wanted to visit at the hospital, and Adam said no. When he arrived home that afternoon his mother came over and said, "Your father is dead."

Adam rushed and nearly knocked over his uncle. Then he fell on the floor weeping, crying, "Bring him back. Bring him back. Bring him back."

Finally, exhausted and weak, Adam stopped. Death in the afternoon. For Adam there were two deaths, his father's and his own.

Adam came to me a year and a half later.

This chapter is, in part, a musing on (in?) countertransference. It is also about the power and limits of transference and the therapeutic work of becoming real. It is about doubt, hesitation, and despair, which should never leave an analyst for a moment. It is about the agony of bringing another to see and accept the unacceptable, the agony which tells us that we really have come to care and to love. It is part history and part notes to myself.

But mostly this chapter is for Adam, the son I could never have, from the daddy he could never have.

"Do you want an apple, mooshki?"
"I'll have my usual, daddy."

Adam O.

Adam was first referred to me because he had asked to go to boarding school and his mother was not sure if such a move would be good for him. Since his father's death their relationship had steadily deteriorated; Adam had become increasingly hard to handle. He insisted on doing as he pleased, refused to listen to his mother, and settled most arguments by announcing that he was leaving home. He often did leave, slamming the door behind him, but always eventually returned. His mother, however, often did not know where he was, and constantly worried. She was depressed and weak herself, and felt no match for a large and strong adolescent. She awoke each morning nervously worrying when the next fight would take place.

It seemed as if his moving away from home would be a welcome respite for both of them.

In the initial sessions, Adam was extremely, even overly, friendly and talkative. He spoke enthusiastically of his friends, his drum playing, and an endless list of past and present girlfriends. He confided that he had lost his virginity within a few days of his fourteenth birthday and then catalogued all of the rest of his heterosexual adventures for me.

He also spoke briefly of school, where he was not working up to potential, and sadly of his father. Somewhat surprisingly it turned out that Adam had been adopted at birth by Mr. and Mrs. O., although Mr. O. had been, then, in his late fifties. But it was clear that Adam stood in awe of his father, a multilingual European refugee who had become a success in his adopted country. They had apparently been very close, and Mr. O.'s death had been a great blow to Adam.

The depth of their bond, with its hopeless (cruel?)

promise of continuity, became clear to me in the minutes just after a session (how often the truth comes after the session ends!) in which Adam had spoken longingly of his father. As he rose from his seat to leave I heard him humming a song and I asked what it was.

"It's a very sad song," he replied, "called 'Time After Time'."

Adam's early development had been normal and unremarkable. But when he was nine, just after an intense attachment to his father had begun, the apartment was burglarized.

Adam sat in his parents' bedroom doing his homework when suddenly two men rushed into the room. They tied up Adam and Mr. and Mrs. O. One man pointed a gun at them and said, "If you make any noise I'll kill you."

Terrified, Adam buried his head into his mother's body and cried without allowing himself to make any noise.

When the burglars left, Mr. O. untied Adam and he then untied his mother. But the damage had been done. Adam saw his father, a strong and strapping man, reduced to helplessness. His mother was suddenly powerless to comfort him. In one instant he saw how easily he could lose his whole world and all of its support. He trembled if he saw similar men in the street. He became terrified of sleeping alone and slept with his parents for months.

It was his first traumatic experience of loss.

Since a decision was needed within a few weeks, I decided to do a limited amount of psychological testing in an attempt to see if there appeared to be any major pathology lurking beneath the exterior of this otherwise handsome, gregarious, and charming young man.

Intelligence testing revealed a superior cognitive capacity, although there were indications of poor school performance, poor attention span, and immaturity. The Rorschach protocol suggested that Adam was having difficulty separating sex and aggression and, indeed, seemed to have trouble perceiving any cooperation between people or animals.[1] There also appeared a large amount of controlled anger. But, most surprisingly, in light of his apparently successful and exciting sexual adventures, was his rejection of Card VI[2] ("I can't make anything out of this one") and his offering, after prompting, of a response that suggested depression and introspection.

I called the school which had accepted Adam and they sent me material about their program. The following week I had a long talk with the school about Adam. It seemed to be the right type of school for him, at least as I understood his needs. It was small, community oriented, and coed, and seemed to have the time and staff to care about each youngster. So, after more thought, and discussion with Adam, I called his mother and recommended that she go ahead with the plans to send him away in the fall. It seemed like the best decision for Adam as well as his mother. He was still fighting with her incessantly, and a move away from home might give them the break that they both needed from each other.

---

[1] For example, "Two dogs biting each other with blood coming out" in response to Card II, "Two women fighting over a man" in response to Card III, and "Two spiders fighting over their food" in response to Card X.

[2] Card VI is usually considered to be the "sex" card of the Rorschach.

The next few weeks did not provide any further insight into Adam, although it became clear why his father's death had been such an enormous loss for him. Apparently realizing that he was terminally ill, Mr. O. devoted endless amounts of time in his last three years to Adam. Mrs. O. took a back seat to a relationship which became intense and which eventually excluded her. Since Mr. O. wanted to leave an indelible memory of himself with Adam, to the extent possible they became inseparable. They ate together, pretended together, stayed up late together talking. When Mrs. O. tried to impose some structure on Adam, his father would step in on his behalf, saying, "Let him do what he wants. Life is short. They only have one childhood." While it was clear that Adam stood in awe of his father, it became equally clear how much Mr. O. adored Adam. Letters to the almost twelve-year-old Adam at summer camp are addressed to "My son — My slutky Mooshki"[3] or "My beloved Son." And so Adam was drawn inexorably closer, never realizing that with each passing day he was becoming more and more attached to a phantom.

From my notes — April

A strange one, this one. He alternates between the real (and what a real fourteen-year-old he is) and the ethereal. And then, where is he?

In the beginning all I could see was his dancing, dancing away, dancing around. The spider whose web is hid-

---

[3]Slutky Mooshki is a Serbo-Croatian endearment meaning "my sweet little one."

den in the shadows; you don't see it, but you know it's there.

Has the road to Hell ever been paved with better intentions? The intense relationship with his father in the last three years caused two great losses, first the loss of a good and close relationship with his mother, and then, of course, the loss of the father. And Adam, poor Adam, left with his closest relationships broken or lost to him.

The early difficulties with his mother prove a godsend to me; in his talking it is clear that he has taken over as "man of the house" (he even tells her of his sexual exploits, as if to say, "See, I am a man"). So their real trouble together is his denial of her new role in the home. And then a fight between them causes Adam to run away. He stays overnight at the office and his hysteria about homosexuality surfaces. What am I to make of it? And his rejection of Card VI in the Rorschach (and later depressive response to it)? The further I pursue it, the more he fights me. First, if I am gay he will walk out. Second, if he finds out that he is gay he will kill himself.

I guess I did not react as he expected to his threats. He confides his difficulty in talking about the subject to his mother and more hysteria develops. She calls me the next day and repeats his suicide threat. Through her tears I hear, unmistakably, "*Don't* talk about this anymore." He is manipulating me through her, or at least trying. If I allow it, it will destroy the analysis.

Finally, Papa Freud comes to my aid. In trying to discuss why he does not want to talk about homosexuality, Adam slips and says, "You don't understand. It's just that I'm not comfortable with *other* homosexuals." So, what to make of such a crucial Freudian slip from a youngster with an entirely heterosexual background? It leads to wonder; perhaps his heterosexuality is defensive, or disguised bisexuality?

149

It turns out that his father was quite anti-gay.[4] What else did Adam hear? And what was his sexual bent when he heard it? What of himself did he submerge in order to be the son his father wanted? What will happen if he discovers he is not totally what he has represented himself to be? And what to do with his probably submerged sexuality? Who knows what mother nature intended him to be? If I leave it all alone, and he is other than what he appears, then I am guilty of the worst negligence—cheating him of his true sexuality and joy. And yet it causes him such agony; lately, whenever it is the subject of conversation I feel the tension so acutely that I begin to tremble. God help me.

The main problem and work for me is, of course, the attachment disorder. What he longs for most, he also fears most. Finally, it begins to come out. He has really not accepted that his father is dead. He is playing, unconsciously, with the idea of transference. And yet, how ambivalent he must feel about it. He hits me a lot; he loves being loved by me, but hates the fact that it is me and not his father. And yet he, in our play fights, always lets me take the father's role and defeat him, even though he is stronger than I.

He is terrified of becoming close to anyone anymore. "I just don't want it to ever happen again. I just don't want anyone to leave me again." And yet, of course, being close again is just what he wants most. "What I miss most is being loved and cherished." And finally, "I love you." And yet, of course, it is still only that I love him. He *needs* me, which is quite different. What will happen when he goes away? When I suggest that he may need, and therefore

---

[4]Both Adam and his mother independently recalled that Mr. O's ultimate insult was to refer to someone as a "stupid faggot."

find, others to talk to when he is away, he weeps and says he wants only me.

Freudian slips begin to appear with reference to the transference. At lunch on Saturday he slips, asking, "What're you going to order, Dad?" It is *instantly blocked* from his mind, and when I pointed out what he had said, he seemed quite taken aback.[5]

So now the webbing feels firmly under my feet and we are like two spiders eyeing each other warily. He barely knows me and vice versa. Will he let us both see what is really there? I must know him fully so that he comes to know that it is the real Adam that I love. And as for you, you trickster, you are indeed subtle, but hopefully you are not mean.[6]

As April moved on, Adam and I increased our sessions from once to twice a week. And as I continued to discuss the problems at home and their possible relationship to his denial of his father's death, another difficulty arose. Since Adam was afraid of anyone ever leaving him again, he had learned how to ingratiate himself with others at all times. If they angered him, he ignored his anger, burying it deep inside; if they were insensitive and tread near his rage, he

[5]In the car with his mother and me, Adam teasingly says that he knows how old I am. In mock seriousness, I said, "Uh, uh, you mustn't tell."

He then quickly says, "Rick is 73."

Immediately struck with the significance of the number, I said, "What an interesting number that is."

Adam looked confused, but his mother quickly understood, and asked him, "How old would daddy be if he were alive today?" Adam was very surprised when he realized what the answer really was.

[6]"Raffiniert is der Herr Gott, aber boshaft ist er nicht." "The Lord is subtle (tricky), but he is not mean." — Albert Einstein

laughed. I began to see this mechanism in operation during our sessions. The closer I came to the pain, the more he laughed. It was frightening and hysterical laughter, too, the laughter of terror.[7]

Finally, I could bear it no longer. When I broached a subject which caused him to laugh in this way, I refused to stop. Tears came to his eyes and he begged me to shut up. He threatened to hit me, and I replied that I didn't care; he had to stop laughing and bottling up the anger. He was killing himself. I got out of my chair and leaned over him on the couch. He laughed and cried more and had that terrible terrified look on his face that children often do when they think they are going to be struck. I kept on and he jumped up from the sofa and tried to pull me down on the floor. I resisted being pulled down for a few minutes because I wanted to bring his rage to the surface as fully as possible. Then suddenly I let go, and he flung me onto the floor and jumped on top of me. Immediately he began to choke me to death, as, unconsciously at least, he must have realized that a person who cannot breathe cannot speak either, and so he will finally silence me.

But just as suddenly, the reality of what he was doing hit him, and he stopped choking me, terrified of his own desire to hurt me. I yelled at him to face how much he hates, inside himself, and he burst into tears. "I don't want to hurt you. I wasn't going to kill you. I don't want to hurt

---

[7]His terror of rage went both ways and was mixed with frightening, magical thinking. "I don't let anyone get close because I'm afraid I'll hurt them." And later — "I spent so much time with my dad and he died; maybe if I spend a lot of time with you something will happen to you, too. Maybe you'll die." "I don't get close to anyone because I'm afraid they'll hurt me."

anybody." Over and over again. But this was not true, and I made him face it; I made him face how much he hated that his father was dead, that his mother had survived, and that it was now me, and not his father, on whom he has come to rely for love and cherishing.

And he got up on the couch again, crying more quietly now, and began to acknowledge how far he had shut himself off from the world. He begged me to help him. "I want to love again. I want to be angry again. I just want to be normal again." And I hugged him and held him, and at last we left the office, hand in hand, and I drove him home.

From my notes — May

In the car, on the way home, I was talking gently to Adam, and he was answering softly, mostly by saying "Mmhmm" to signal agreement. It suddenly struck me that he might not actually be paying attention at all; I asked, deliberately in the negative, "It seems that you are not really listening to me at all. Is that so?"

And, hearing the pause for an answer, he replied, "Mmhmm."

I stopped the car in surprise and asked him if he realized what he had just said. And when I explained his response he admitted that I was correct and said, sadly, that he has *not listened* to anyone since his father died.

God, he has not really heard anything since his father died (does not want to hear another voice — perhaps a contradictory voice?). So, he is an as-if personality, to some extent. With me he is what he thinks *I* expect a good patient to be; with girls he is macho (for his father's sake?); with friends, superficial. I, then, don't know anything about him at all for certain, since everything he has told me may be just what he thinks I want to hear! He *acts as if* he is a good patient and is, therefore, because he is acting, in fact a terrible patient.

Perhaps he feels that in some way he was not what his biological parents wanted (and was too young to find out what it was and, therefore, how to fake it) and *so* they gave him away. *Now* he finds out what you want and acts it for you so *you* won't give him away. Maybe that is why when he is with me he is so close (he knows I value closeness) but becomes so distant when he is away from me. The strands of the web feel like they have become stainless steel.

Adam rejects this "chameleon" interpretation outright and angrily. So, perhaps it is incorrect. Then why does the intensity of our relationship disappear when he is not with me? If attachment is the whole explanation, then he is close with me when he is at the office because then I am there and alive, but when he is away from me perhaps I have disappeared. It is all right to be intense when he can touch me and see me, but when he is not there with me it is too dangerous; I might cease to exist and he would be hurt. After all, he says of his father, "He wasn't supposed to die."

On the way out of the office Adam asks if I will adopt him. Then he will have a mother and a father. "Now it's just me and my mom."

Poor, poor, Adam. How I would love to adopt you if it would help. What a beautiful son you would make. And yet, tricky one, is this what you intended when you brought him into my life?

Both interpretations of Adam seem correct. The attachment disorder has developed since his father's death and expresses itself in his chameleon-like approach to adults now. He says, "I want everyone to love me. I don't want anyone to be angry with me."

And I reply that since nobody *knows* him, *nobody* really loves him at all.

Did his father really know him? Or did he also love a phantom? More talk of his father's death reveals that, lying in bed, he daydreams for hours of his father knocking on his bedroom door and returning. He says, "I still can't believe I'll never see him again."

He not only did not see him on that last, fatal day, but remembers pleading with his mother to allow him to look in the coffin, and being turned down. I sadly tell Adam that there is a final conversation missing between him and his father. I know I must get to this with him, but I do not know how. And if I find out how, will I have the strength?

Despair. How can I make him see the unseeable? Time. There just isn't enough. What will I do? Give up? Never. Push on? Where to? He doesn't even want to.

June began and I realized that only four weeks were left before Adam was to leave for summer camp. I had so far to go with him but there was so little time left. I resolved to push myself as I knew I must. Adam and I had continued to grow closer. He invited me to his confirmation, gave me "the best ticket," and invited me out to lunch with his family after the ceremony.

I realized that as a beginning I would have to tackle the father's death by going to the cemetery. Adam had only been there twice in two years, at the funeral, of course, and at the unveiling of the headstone. I mentioned this idea to his mother, and she agreed. We set a date.

Adam also began to be able to discuss his sexuality. His early hysteria subsided to a quiet but nervous acknowledgment that it was an area which had to be explored. At first this exploration was intellectual and informational; he asked me all sorts of questions about homosexuality. But, as time went on he began to admit to his own attraction to men, first from a purely aesthetic point of view, but finally, from a sexual one as well.

We talked at length of accepting this part of his sexuality, and he worried that none of his friends would be able to accept it, let alone himself. Constantly he wanted to know if he was only homosexual, or bisexual, or heterosexual. And I replied over and over that I did not know; reality would show him. I would accept him.

June 13

It begins to seem clear that the part of Adam that resists allowing him to become really a part of the world again also resists believing that his father is genuinely dead. So the question I have been asking myself in these last two weeks is how to bring Adam face to face with his father's death, how to help him to accept the unacceptable, so that he can begin to grieve, so that he can begin to feel the longing and put it to rest.

I searched through some prayer books and found a short prayer, addressed to God, written for mourners.[8] It

[8]This is the text of the prayer as we used it:

> O God, help me to live with my grief!
> Death has taken my father and I feel that I cannot go on.
> My faith is shaken; my mind keeps asking: Why? Why does joy end in sorrow?
> Why does love exact its price in tears? Why?

seems to address Adam's questions: Why? Why did my father die? Why did God let my father die? And I altered the prayer so that it read "death has taken my father" instead of "death has taken my beloved."

Toward the end of the session today I took out the prayer and my large prayer shawl and Adam and I both huddled under it, and I asked Adam to read the prayer. The first time through he read it very mechanically, partly not knowing the words and partly trying to keep it from being emotional. I asked him to read it through again, but that reading was also very empty. Finally, I said, "Adam, read it like you're talking to God instead of like you're reading words." And then he started to read again, altering the initial line so that it read, "O God, *please* help me to live with my grief," instead of just "O God, help me to live with my grief." When he got to the second line ("Death has taken my father . . . ") it was quite clear that the emotion of the prayer had reached him.

June 20

In spite of Adam's resistance, I have arranged to take him and his mother to the cemetery where his father is

---

O God, help me to live with my grief!
Help me to accept the mystery of life.
Help me to see that even if my questions were answered, even if I did know why,
the pain would be no less, the loneliness would remain bitter beyond words.
Still my heart would ache.
O God, help me to triumph over my grief!

(Original prayer by Rabbi Robert I. Kahn in Stern, Chaim (Ed.), *Gates of Prayer The New Union Prayerbook*. New York: Central Conference of American Rabbis, 1975, p. 624.)

buried. I arrived early in the morning to pick them up, and his mother came down first with a bag full of letters written to Adam when he was in camp in 1981. The letters were from Adam's father as well as other people, and the bag also contained some tapes which hopefully will have some recordings of Adam's father on them.

Adam appeared a few minutes after his mother and was obviously very angry and upset. Since we had to stop by my office, I double-parked my car and asked Adam to come in to get a drink since he had had nothing for breakfast. But really I tried to use the opportunity of having him in the office to say that if he was angry or upset that it would be good to get it out then. Adam denied being angry although he then quickly left the office without waiting for me.

On the way to the cemetery his anger became increasingly clear, and yet when we finally got there he was the one who knew exactly where his father was buried and gave me directions.

Before we climbed up to the gravesite I confronted Adam with his anger and told him that the purpose of being at the cemetery would be defeated unless he could get over some of his anger toward me. Adam said he was ashamed to yell in the cemetery but did acknowledge that he hated me for bringing him and didn't understand why we had come.

I said then that we should go up to the gravesite. So we went to where his mother was sitting and we both sat down also. And then his mother talked about his father and about his father's sister who is also buried there, and about his father's parents who are also buried there. After a while I took out the prayers I had brought for Adam and myself, but Adam said that he was not going to read them, and I told him that he must. And he said to me, "I don't like to be here because I know that my father's body is in there," and I said, "I know, Adam."

Then his mother said, "Should I go away?" And Adam said no, just as I said yes, and his mother got up to leave.[9] I think that Adam was very shocked that his mother listened to me and not to him because he said, "Ma, didn't you hear me? I said no." And his mother replied, "Yes, but Rick is the one who is helping us, so I'm going to do what he says."

After his mother left Adam and I read some of the prayers, but true to his word, as if punishing me and himself, he did not cry or allow himself to become emotional. Then I said to him, "Adam, now you talk to your father and I'll talk to my friend Elisabeth."

He seemed quite surprised and asked, "Is Elisabeth buried here, too?"

And I said, "No, but she is here in just the same way that your father is here because he is alive in you and Elisabeth is alive in me."

We stayed like that, silent, for a while, and Adam began to cry, and so did I. Then he stood up and said, "I can't stay here anymore." I gave him my hand to help me up, and then we hugged each other.

[9]I felt that he would be able to express his grief without her there; he had confided that he hid his tears from her because he knew how depressed she already was.

From my notes — June

As the sessions and the time we spend together increases dramatically in these last two weeks before Adam is going to camp, the difficulty that he is having in his relationship with me becomes more and more apparent. When he is with me the relationship vacillates from the superficial to the enormously intense, and yet as soon as he leaves the office it is as if I and the relationship become shadowy mists that seem to lose their reality, their force, and their effect. And yet I know I am present within him because in trouble, in need, in pain, he always calls, he always reaches out to me.

June 22

Adam was supposed to be without an allowance this weekend but asked his mother for next week's allowance in advance. She called me and since there seemed some logic to the fact that next week's allowance will do very little good next week because he will be in camp she agreed to give it to him.

But while we were on the phone the other phone kept ringing with various friends of Adam calling up. When he was finally ready to go out his mother suggested that he invite a friend along and they got into an argument about her butting into his personal life. Adam flew off the handle and started to call his mother all sorts of names, and then, when he finished, still asked for his allowance. She, of course, correctly felt that he must be out of his mind if he thought he could insult her that way and then ask for money. She told him she wasn't going to give him anything, and he left and said that he was never coming back.

Adam O.

Adam called me at midnight and we stayed on the phone for about an hour. His mother had called me earlier to discuss how she would punish him and had finally decided to remove his stereo, his drumsticks so that he could not play his drums, and his telephone, as well as keeping his allowance from him. The punishment was to last for the weekend. We agreed to meet on Saturday, the three of us, to try to discuss the argument that they had had.

In terms of transference, Adam had, from the beginning, treated me very much as an authority, and as a safe and available harbor. And yet part of him resisted genuinely allowing me to be "real" for him. His terror of loving me, and letting me love him, and becoming vulnerable again to loss, brought to my mind Ernest Becker's understanding of the transference.

> This is how we can understand the essence of transference: as a *taming of terror*. Realistically the universe contains overwhelming power. Beyond ourselves we sense chaos. We can't really do much about this unbelievable power, except for one thing: we can endow certain persons with it. The child takes natural awe and terror and focuses them on individual beings, which allows him to find the power and the horror all in one place instead of diffused throughout a chaotic universe. *Mirabile!* The transference object, being endowed with the transcendent powers of the universe, now has in himself the power to control, order, and combat them. . . .
>
> This totality of the transference object also helps explain its ambivalence. In some complex ways the child has to fight against the power of the parents in their awesome

miraculousness. They are just as overwhelming as the background of nature from which they emerge. The child learns to naturalize them by techniques of accommodation and manipulation. At the same time, however, he has to focus on them the whole problem of terror and power, making them the center of it in order to cut down and naturalize the world around them. Now we see why the transference object poses so many problems. The child does partly control his larger fate by it, but it becomes his new fate. He binds himself to one person to automatically control terror, to mediate wonder, and to defeat death by that person's strength. But then he experiences "transference terror"; the terror of losing the object, of displeasing it, of not being able to live without it. The terror of his own finitude and impotence still haunts him, but now in the precise form of the transference object. How implacably ironic is human life. The transference object always looms larger than life size because it represents all of life and hence all of one's fate. The transference object becomes the focus of the problem of one's freedom because one is compulsively dependent on it; it sums up all other natural dependencies and emotions. . . .

No wonder Freud could say that transference was a "universal phenomenon of the human mind" that "dominates the whole of each person's relation to his human environment." Or that Ferenczi could talk about the "neurotic passion for transference," the "stimulus-hungry affects of neurotics." . . . We might better say that transference proves that everyone is neurotic, as it is a universal distortion of reality by the artificial fixation of it. It follows, of course, that the less ego power one has and the more <u>fear</u>, the stronger the transference.[10]

[10]Becker, E. *The Denial of Death*. New York: Free Press, 1973, pp. 145–147. (Italics in the original, underlining added by the author)

Transference develops; it grows; it changes. It doesn't happen at one special moment, and yet, for Adam, our next session was critical in just that way. Suddenly in the next session I became, at last, real.

༃

June 23

All the way to the office I kept on asking myself, "What am I going to do with Adam?" I had five days left to make our relationship real so that he could not just exchange me for someone else like a person using Kleenex to blow his nose. How could I help him to accept all of the things that he had denied? — that I am real, that his mother is now the person who runs the house, that his father is dead, that in his own personality and in his own sexuality he may not be what he pretends to be, to himself and to others.

And suddenly I was struck with the idea, it came to me more or less as an image in my mind, of bringing his father back. At first, I imagined what I would do if I were a real sorcerer. I saw myself conjuring up the shade of Adam's father. And I played through several conversations between the two of them in my mind. In each I put words into Mr. O.'s mouth, trying to imagine what magic words would finally help Adam.

Then, sadly, I came back to reality (after my fantasied triumphs) and wondered what I would do since I was not a magician. I saw Adam and his mother seated on the sofa together and myself seated in my chair, and I saw an empty chair. And suddenly I felt that that was what I must do.

Adam arrived a half an hour before his mother, as arranged, and he and I discussed the incidents of Friday night. Then, when his mother arrived but was still in the waiting room, I said, "Adam, you will sit here and your mother will sit on the other side of the sofa, and I will sit in my chair, and this fourth chair is for your father."

Adam was very startled and said, "What do you mean?"

And I replied, "Because this is an issue between you and your mother, and for you your father is still very much alive and available for comment, I want him to be here too."

Then we brought Mrs. O. in, and I didn't say anything to her about the chair or the meaning of the chair. At first they discussed the incidents of Friday night and were sort of fighting verbally back and forth, yelling at each other, yelling over each other.

But then, after about a half an hour, Adam began to look to the chair, and the entire course of the conversation changed. It shifted entirely away from the events of Friday night and his punishment. Adam started to talk to his father, not quite out loud, but in sort of a silent, lip-moving soto voce. And I kept asking him, "What are you saying?" and he would say, "I'm asking my dad how he is and he says he's happy but he's sad. And I ask him for help and he tells me he cannot help me because he's in Heaven and I'm here." Then Adam said how much he missed his father and how much he wants to be with him, and then interjected quite suddenly, "It's not that I want to kill myself; it's just that sometimes I can't wait to die so that I can be with him again." Then he went on to ask what the point is in living when he really just wants to be dead so that he can be with his father again.

And then quite abruptly the subject lost its emotional

tone and became an intellectual discussion, with Adam asking me if I believe in Heaven or Hell, and where do bad people go if there is no Heaven or Hell? I explained to him my own beliefs, and he said, "Maybe that's so; nobody knows." And I agreed with him that nobody knows. And then he said sometimes he doubts that there is a Heaven and sometimes he doubts that there is even a God.

He started talking to his father again and I saw him smiling and he told me his father was reminding him of good times they had in the past, and he started to relate some of the good times down in Florida on vacation. His mother smiled too, and I asked Adam what his father said to his mother.

And Adam said, "My father says he cannot hear my mother."

So I said, "Isn't that because you don't want him to hear your mother?"

And Adam said, "No. He's angry because he can't hear my mother." But I insisted that it was that Adam didn't want his father to hear his mother. And then finally he said, "Yes, I'm making him deaf."

Then the subject became emotional again. I began to see Adam's rage coming up again. The rage that he still only partially acknowledged: that he hates his mother for surviving; that he hates it that his father is dead; and, as still yet unacknowledged in Adam, that he hates his father for dying and leaving him. I urged Adam to reach into his rage and to let it out, but again the terror that he will hurt and kill his mother was much too great for him and he tried to restrain the anger. He squeezed the little stuffed toy that I had given him to hold during the session and he said to it, "It's a good thing that this doesn't hurt you."

The rage was still there on the surface and I tried to push him to express it, sitting on the edge of my chair realizing that I might have to leap up and prevent him from hitting his mother. The rage was so great that almost every muscle in Adam's body went stiff in his effort to control it. And then Adam made one massive effort, and you could almost *see* all of the anger being sucked into the little box where he keeps it inside of himself. And then he swallowed and broke out in a sweat and said, "It's gone now."

I saw for myself that it was gone, and yet there was still a tingling left on the surface, so I worked with that, encouraging it to come back, trying to get him to acknowledge the loss and the pain. He started to ask again, "Why? Why did my father die? It's unfair." And I saw the anger beginning to come up again and I agreed with him that yes, it was unfair, as many things in life are unfair. And he asked me again, "Why? Why?"

And I said to him, "Adam, remember our prayer. The prayer says that even if we knew why, even if we understood why, it wouldn't help, it wouldn't make us less bitter or less lonely." And this reminder of the prayer seemed to push Adam over a certain threshold within himself and he took one of the small pillows from the sofa and he fell down on the carpet in front of the wooden chair and he grabbed onto the legs of it and wept. And I realized that for him the chair *had* brought back the reality of his father, who was there for him, alive for him, not at all, in any sense, gone. And I let Adam weep and then I said, getting up and grasping the chair from the top, "I think that it's time for me to take this chair back to where it belongs."

I picked up the chair and brought it back in front of the computer where it belonged. When I turned around,

Adam was still on the floor weeping with his right arm outstretched, grasping for the chair. And so I went back to him and leaned down, holding him and listening to him say over and over, "Bring it back. Bring it back. Bring it back."

And I said to Adam, "Why don't you ask for what you really want?" And he said, "Bring him back. Bring him back. Bring him back." And I replied, "That's just it Adam. I can't bring him back, and nobody else can either."

He continued to weep and then he got up on his knees and held onto me and cried on me, and then finally turned away to get some tissues to dry his tears. Then he reached back for me and moved forward to kiss me. I gave him my cheek, but he took his hand and moved my face around to kiss me on the lips. So it was clear that he wanted his mother to see that for whatever his reasons.

In the next few minutes the reason that he kissed me on the mouth in front of his mother became very clear. The phone rang and I went to put on the answering machine so we would not be disturbed. When I turned around, Adam was standing by the air conditioner letting cool air blow up his shirt. I walked over to him to see if he was all right. And he said to me in a whisper, "My mother is jealous of us; I can see it in her look, I can hear it in her tone." I was suddenly struck by the fact that in kissing me Adam was recreating for his mother the very kind of divisiveness that existed in their household in the last three years that his father was alive, except that it would be he and I now in a relationship which excluded his mother. How the transference recreates pathology before our very eyes! This feeling was further reinforced a couple of minutes later as we were leaning against the bookcase, he and

I standing together, his mother ten feet away on the sofa. And Adam whispered to me, "I want you to tell my mother that I want you to adopt me." I told him that I was not going to tell her that; as if to reassure me that this is what he still wanted and that it was real for him, he said, "You know that still holds, don't you?"

And I said, "Yes Adam, I do know that that still holds. I know that you want to become as close to me as you can, but the relationship you had with your father wasn't good for you or your mother and making another one like it with me wouldn't be good either."

Adam accepted this quietly and the session came to an end.

In the evening Adam had another confrontation with his mother. He brought two friends home and wanted to play the drums for them, but unfortunately he was without drumsticks until Monday morning. When his mother refused to give them to him for even five minutes he lost his temper and started calling her names and taking things out of her room. His mother naturally got very upset and walked out into the hall, saying that she could not tolerate that behavior anymore. Her current boyfriend, Harold, remained in the apartment with Adam and his two friends. Harold yelled and screamed at Adam for the way he was treating his mother. Adam became completely hysterical and left the house. He called me but I had gone out to dinner, so he just left a message. When I got home, I called him but his answering machine was on, so I assumed that everything was all right.

Adam O.

June 24, 2:45 A.M.

Adam called me and carried on for an hour about how Harold had yelled at him and had threatened to hit him. And how that wasn't right since Harold wasn't his father. Adam confronted his mother and said that he wanted her to stop seeing Harold; if she didn't, he would never come home again. I pointed out to Adam that I did not think that that was an appropriate request, that his mother was entitled to her love life. I tried to explain to him that, although I felt that he was correct that Harold had erred in yelling at him and threatening him, Harold was a human being and human beings make mistakes. And I asked him to try to see that part of his own pathology was that the first time a person crosses him he just throws them away.

By Sunday the situation had calmed down substantially. I spoke to Mrs. O. on the phone and tried to point out to her that I hoped the session on Saturday had demonstrated to her how very fragile Adam still is underneath his very polished, superficial veneer of social competence. It is unfortunate that this rather attractive veneer, coupled with Adam's musical talent, as well as good looks, dovetail so neatly into his pathology of forming many superficial, meaningless relationships. I think that by the time I finished, she had begun to clearly understand how much Adam has killed of himself since his father died.

From my notes — June

To a certain extent it appears that from the moment he found out that his father had died part of Adam got

169

shut up and also died. He is still in shock. He still doesn't accept his father's death, and until he does he cannot go on with his own life. Nothing can be alive within him because there is no point to living.

It suddenly occurred to me that all of Adam's problems are related. Because he shut himself off at the age of twelve when his father died, he has also shut himself off from developing more sophisticated defenses than the few available in childhood. And so, he still relies quite heavily on the major defense of childhood—denial. The common denominator of all Adam's problems is denial. He denies that his father is dead and therefore he cannot go on living. He denies that his mother is now running the home and therefore he engages in endless battles with her for control. He denies that he is either homosexual or bisexual and therefore his sexuality remains heterosexual, but compulsive and meaningless. [11] He denies that our relationship is real

---

[11] As therapy continued into a second year, it became clearer that the attachment disorder also figured significantly in Adam's compulsive heterosexuality. Either because of an unconscious certainty as to his own "badness" or a similarly unconscious certainty that if a woman loves you she will then reject you (his biological mother gave him up, after all), he uses his good looks and charm to seduce, confusing "making love" with "being loved," and then manipulates things so that the girl breaks off with him. So, each new "love" is described as "really nice" and yet the relationships quickly fall apart, almost always within a few days of the first intercourse. In addition, his manipulations are earning him the reputation, he unconsciously wants, as a shallow, callous "bastard."

This became clear to me on one of the occasions when Adam asked me if I would help him to search for his biological mother when he became old enough. I pointed out to him that he only asks to search for his mother, never his father. He became stonily angry and practically yelled, "I don't have a father."

When I pointed out that obviously he did, he yelled again, "I don't care about him. Don't you understand? They weren't married when they had me. I'm a bastard!"

so that he will not be faced with the terror of either losing me and being hurt himself, or of killing me and thereby also losing me and being hurt. So, for our last week together our sessions and time together must be different than they have been in the past. Adam must come to see that his fear of losing me is not really real, because you cannot lose someone you do not have.

June 25

When Adam came to the office this morning, I told him my thoughts. And I told him that if he doesn't want to lose me that he will have to come and get me. He asked me to help him, but I told him that any way that I suggest would be my way, and he has to find his own way to become real with me. He agonized with this throughout the very long time that we were together. He sat in the chair and said, "You don't know how badly I want you." And yet there is a part of him that is still fighting desperately against it.

When we got to the subject of his sexuality, he looked at me, tired, perhaps, and weakened, and pleaded with me, "I don't want to be gay." Why say that if it isn't so possible? And so I told him that it's not up to him to want it; we are what we are. He has to look in himself and face what he is, and stop denying, denying, denying. Denying me, denying his mother, denying himself.

June 26

I have four more days left with Adam. Four more days of trying to bring him to accept a relationship which is based on who he really is and who I really am so that all the work of the last four months will not be in vain. I am anxious to see how he will progress in these next four days as the moment of our leaving each other comes closer and closer. How will he handle his goodbyes? What commitments will he be capable of making for the future?

And as for you, tricky one, I am beginning to see a pattern in the demands you make on me.

I took Adam and his mother to see him off to camp. It was pouring that day, and when it finally was time for him to board the bus our farewells were mercifully short. He looked happy and excited as he climbed up the steps, not even turning around to wave goodbye.

A few days later he called; he was at the local hospital having a throat culture done to see if he had a strep infection. But he sounded in good spirits, told me he already had a girlfriend, and confided that he had not quit smoking as the camp required. I asked him what the punishment was if he was caught, and he replied, "Expulsion." I asked him if he wanted to get thrown out and he said no, so I told him that then he must not do things if he could not live with their consequences. He asked me if I had written to him and said that he would write back as soon as he received my letter.

In fact, he did. His first letter sounded happy and had only one brief sentence relating to our separation.

"I'm having a great time here, but It would be great If I could see you."

Shortly after receiving that letter, I wrote back and let Adam know that I would be leaving to visit my eldest daughter in Boston and would then be in Cape Cod for a few days. While I was gone, in a period spanning just nine days, nine additional letters arrived from Adam. Had I even seen the third or fourth before I left, perhaps I could have prevented Adam from carrying out his plan.

The letters began to deteriorate in tone, and the separation difficulties became the larger focus. From the second letter:

I really miss you. . . . I love you so much and I miss you more than anyone.

And from the third:

I don't know why but I really want to come home. You know If I <u>really</u> [in the letter this "really" was triply underlined] wanted to come I could get thrown out of here. I might.

From the fourth:

Dear Rick (Daddy),
I still want you to adopt me, so I can call you dad! I miss you so much. The [present] that you will give me will be worth nothing compared to your love. . . . I hope to God that you can come up. Most of my friends know that you are my shrink. I love you so much.

From the seventh:

If I ever want to go home I hope you will help me.

On the 18th of July, the anniversary of Adam's father's death, he called me in Cape Cod. He was on a camp day trip and was obviously unhappy. He asked me if I had been reading his letters and told me that he had been writing every day; it was the first inkling I had that things might be very bad with him. I told him that I had not been in my office since I had received his first letter but that I was looking forward to reading all of his wonderful letters.

And then he asked me if I knew what the day was, and I told him that I did. It must have been so hard for him, missing his father so much and having me only on the phone and so far away. I talked to him gently and tried to ease his pain, and, of course, I told him that I loved him.

The next day I returned to New York, and in the evening I stopped by my office and picked up my mail. I put Adam's letters in order (from the postmarks) and read them with increasing worry until I reached the last one:

> Today I talked with you on the phone. . . . Today I really did not have such a great time (you know why). Oh how I wish you were here with me. I miss you so much. I wish I could lay in your arms and cry. Oh God, Rick, please come and see me at camp. Please, I miss you so much. I beg you on my knees. I think I'm gonna Breakdown and weep if I don't see you soon. I'll cry for a long time. I love you so much. My love for you will never end. Please [quadruply underlined in the letter] come. There are not enough words in the English language to emphasize my need to see you or my need for your intense love. Please come.

It was late at night. I resolved to call Adam the next day and to assure him that somehow I would arrange to come and visit him. But it was not to be. On Saturday afternoon Adam was found smoking and was expelled from camp. By Sunday night he was on the phone with me and set up an appointment for Monday. I told him how sorry I was that he was expelled, but he replied that he was glad to be home. "If I had stayed in camp, all we would have had when I got back was two lousy weeks. Now we'll have seven weeks together before I go to school."

The last week of July raced by, and I was away on vacation the first week of August. Adam had met a boy to whom he admitted he was attracted. It turned out that the attraction was mutual and they began very tentatively to explore sexually with each other. They "made out," as Adam put it, but he said that he had not been aroused by it.

As we discussed this it became clearer to Adam that, at the same time that he admitted that he was attracted, he was trying to deny that he was by not letting himself go.

At our next session he confided that I had been right. He had refused to control himself and discovered that he became fully aroused now when he was kissing his friend. He told me that his friend had wanted to go further but they had been unable to because Adam claimed that several infected hair follicles on his penis were too painful to be touched.

I was skeptical, but Adam swore that it was true. I decided I would call the internist who had first diagnosed the problem and ask his opinion, and, when I did, he assured me that any pain was purely psychosomatic.

August 6

I know now that Adam has lied to me about the pain. Moreover, in spite of the fact that the last time he squeezed one open it became red and more infected, he informed me last night that he had squeezed another one open with the same results. Clearly this seems aimed at creating a reasonable blocking of his homosexual explorations.

When Adam came today I knew that I would have to confront him with this lie. We began by talking about what we each had done in the last ten days; I was in Westhampton; Adam was at home, "hanging out." He had met a new girl with whom he was very taken. Unfortunately, she is a model, and lives in California, and so their relationship, which was beginning to heat up, is destined to be short-lived.

All the while we chatted I was on edge, knowing that I would have to confront Adam, knowing how difficult it would be for him. Finally, unable to hold back anymore, I asked Adam if we could get down to serious business. Then I told him that the pain was psychosomatic, and moreover, that he was, in my opinion, using it to prevent any further progress in terms of his coming to face his sexuality. I did also offer that it might all be unconscious, although I said that I did not believe this as the first explanation was much simpler, to say nothing of more in character.

Adam just sat and shook his head yes, and when I asked him which explanation was correct, he said, "The first one means it was deliberate, but the second one means it wasn't."

I agreed that this was so. He swallowed hard, and I could see how uncomfortable the implication of the whole thing being deliberate was for him. But, after some moments, he started shaking his head yes again, and when I asked what he was shaking about, he said, "You're right; it's the first thing."

But I wanted Adam to say it in his own words and I asked him to do that. But he said, then, "You're right that it was deliberate," still using my words. So I asked him again to put it in his words, and then he said, "I lied. I saw that if I said it hurt he wouldn't push me to do anything, so I said it hurt." There was a short silence. How terrified he must have felt, fighting against himself as to whether or not to own up to the truth, fighting against the fear that I would be angry and hate him, fighting to trust me and my love. But he did trust me and I was so grateful. I told him again, oh how softly, that I still loved him.

And then finally it comes. Why did it come now? Because I was so soft about the lie, because I loved him in spite of the lie? He says, "I had to change myself to be the son my father wanted. Anything for my father's love. I wasn't a chameleon like I am now, because I only had to change once and then stay that way."

I asked him where he had thrown the parts of his personality that didn't fit, and he said that he hadn't thrown them away (we never can—even when we bury them deeply, we are still burying them alive) but rather stuffed them deep inside.

And then, ultimately, as it always had to be, "My father wouldn't have loved me if I had been a homosexual." God how painful it was to realize that. I tried to tell him that I felt he was wrong, that it would have been very difficult for his father but that, in the end, his father would have loved him more than he hated his homosexuality.

He is changing now again ("I'll do anything so that I don't lose you" — again, anything for love), but this time back to himself, little by little, crawling (but maybe someday running) toward the only full love that there can be, the love that loves us *as we are*, the love that lets us look securely, if in fear sometimes, at what we really are, the love that lets us accept ourselves without excusing ourselves, the love that therefore makes us responsible for ourselves and thus, ultimately, free.

Run to yourself, Adam, and love yourself so that I can love you too.

Like all real psychoanalytic relationships, this one is an affair of the heart. So, although it has a beginning, it has no end.

To you then, my dear reader, I can only say:

> The woods are lovely, dark, and deep.
> But I have promises to keep,
> And miles to go before I sleep,
> And miles to go before I sleep. [12]

[12]Frost, R. "Stopping by Woods on a Snowy Evening," in Lathem, E. W. (Ed.), *The Poetry of Robert Frost: The Collected Poems, Complete and Unabridged*. New York: Henry Holt and Company, 1979, pp. 224–225.

Adam O.

And to you, mooshki,

If you're lost, you can look, and you will find me.

Time after time.

If you fall, I will catch you; I'll be waiting.

Time after time.

Time after time.
Time after time.
Time after time.
Time after time.[13]

---

[13]"Time After Time" by Cyndi Lauper and Rob Hyman.